Thoughts and Reflections on Dr. Sternbach and His Work

Dr. Armin Walser, chemist and Sternbach associate and inventor of the injectable sedative Versed

The well-being of his subordinates was always a concern and high priority for Sternbach. While working under his direction, I got to appreciate his many admirable qualities, such as his sense of humor, his contagious optimism and good mood, his modesty and openness. I was particularly impressed by his skill in solving chemistry problems without the now-standard spectroscopic tools. For managers of pharmaceutical research, it is also interesting to emphasize that Sternbach made his big discovery by working on his pet project without the approval of his boss. He knew that Lady Luck had been extremely good to him, not only with the discovery of the benzodiazepines. Nobody seemed to envy him, because he was so well liked and such a nice guy. He liked to share his success with his friends and co-workers. He loved parties and enjoyed food and drink, giving little thought to the calories or the cholesterol content. If I recall correctly, a vodka martini and olive was his favored cocktail and the meat had to be laced with fat. He enjoyed playing Santa at Christmas parties and getting hugged by female admirers. And bridge was his favorite game, beside the stock market.

Dr. Milan Uskokovic, chemist and Sternbach associate, inventor of the vitamin D metabolite Rocaltrol (used by patients with chronic renal failure), and fellow member of the New Jersey Inventors Hall of Fame

By the early 1940s there was a significant migration of European organic medicinal chemists to America in search of opportunities in the rapidly growing field of pharmaceutical research. Leo Sternbach was an outstanding example in this newborn age. In a matter of a year or two after his coming to Roche in Nutley, he accomplished the monumental task of achieving the first total synthesis of the vitamin biotin. His synthesis is still practiced today, almost 60 years later, and is frequently cited as one of the most significant events of natural products synthesis. But that was just the beginning of his growth as a medicinal chemist. He decided to reexamine the chemistry of his student period in Poland and resurrected the benzodiazepines into the most significant series of drugs to combat anxiety, at that time a newly defined mental disorder. He became a grand master of modern medicinal chemistry. He also became a lasting example to all scientists at Roche up to the present time.

Dr. Pius Wehrli, chemist and Sternbach associate, and holder of 17 U.S. patents

Leo Sternbach was an extremely well-trained organic synthesis chemist with a keen ability to observe reactions and draw conclusions based on them. One of his outstanding qualities was his persistence. "Try until you succeed" must have been one of his fundamentals. A truly scientific achievement was his total synthesis of the vitamin biotin. The fact that after over 50 years his process is still commercially used and has not been replaced by a different approach speaks for itself. This is virtually unheard of in synthetic organic chemistry. Dr. Sternbach was well aware that you cannot whip up success at will. It will come at its own pace and often at unexpected moments. The road is full of surprises and predictions are often difficult. Chemistry, and science in general, needs in a certain sense a nonpush atmosphere. That is not to say that chemistry is not pushed, but the push of the true chemist comes from within, and that is what Dr. Sternbach personified.

Good Chemistry

The Life and Legacy of
Valium Inventor Leo Sternbach

Alex Baenninger
Jorge Alberto Costa e Silva
Ian Hindmarch
Hans-Juergen Moeller
Karl Rickels

McGraw-Hill

New York   Chicago   San Francisco   Lisbon   London   Madrid
Mexico City   Milan   New Delhi   San Juan   Seoul
Singapore   Sydney   Toronto

The McGraw·Hill Companies

Library of Congress Cataloging-in-Publication Data
Baenninger, Alex.
  Good chemistry : the life and legacy of valium inventor Leo Sternbach /
by Alex Baenninger.
    p. cm.
  ISBN 0-07-142617-5 (alk. paper)
  1. Sternbach, L. H. (Leo H.) 2. Benzodiazepines—History. 3. Diazepam—History.
4. Chemists—New Jersey—Biography. I. Title.
  RM666.B42S743 2004
  615'.7882—dc21   2003013224

2 3 4 5 6 7 8 9 0   DOC/DOC   0 9 8 7 6 5 4 3

ISBN 0-07-142617-5

Contents

Acknowledgment

Medical writer Bill Breckon worked closely with the four distinguished experts to compile the sections of the book covering the medical and social impact of the benzodiazepines.

Part I

The Biography of Leo Henryk Sternbach

Chapter 1

A Cure for Troubled Souls

Librium is famous, and Valium even more so. Their discovery 40 years ago opened up undreamed-of opportunities for the medical and pharmaceutical worlds. Both medications exhibit the characteristic effects of the benzodiazepines: They are anxiolytics, anticonvulsants, muscle relaxants, and tranquilizers. No previous drugs treated such a range of indications.

The man who discovered the benzodiazepine group of active substances is Leo Henryk Sternbach. His work heralded the start of a new era in research and therapeutics.

The list of Sternbach's extraordinary achievements includes 125 publications, 230 U.S. patents, the Carl Mannich Medal of the German Pharmaceutical Society, the Chemical Pioneer Award of the American Institute of Chemists, induction into the New Jersey Inventors Hall of Fame, and honorary doctorates from the Johann Wolfgang Goethe University, Frankfurt am Main, the University of Vienna, and Centenary College, Hackettstown, New Jersey. *US News & World Report* numbers Sternbach among the 25 most important people of the 20th century, along with Louis Armstrong, Levi Strauss (the inventor of blue jeans), Frank McNamara, (the creator of credit cards), and Charles Houston (the brilliant lawyer who wanted justice for all).

Librium has an international reputation, and Valium is even more widely known. Sternbach, in contrast, has lived his life in the shadow of anonymity. It is a life that should have piqued the curiosity of potential biographers long ago; anyone who rises to the challenge of exploring that life will be rewarded with a tale of suspense and excitement. Sternbach pushed open doors, only to reveal new obstacles. On the heels of recognition came contempt. Periods of a secure and sheltered existence gave way to periods of menace and fear. Scientific breakthroughs triggered political attacks.

At each triumphant step, wisdom dictated modesty. And even in the darkest days of distress, his strength of body and mind bolstered his confidence and optimism.

Sternbach's story is exemplary and simple, shocking and encouraging, fascinating and moving.

Inner Strength

Every day for more than 60 years, Leo Henryk Sternbach, born in 1908, went to work at Roche, the company at which he began his pharmaceutical career in 1940. Even when he stopped driving in the early 1980s, his wife, Herta Sternbach, born 1920, drove her husband to his office daily. It was a 10-minute drive from their single-family home in Upper Montclair, through Bloomfield, to Roche headquarters in Nutley, New Jersey; then she drove him back home again in the early afternoon.

The 10-minute drive through suburban northern New Jersey, 12 miles west of New York, with the skyline of Manhattan in the distance, passed quickly. At intersections the white Chevrolet did not hesitate to claim the right of way; at the security check the car simply slowed to a crawl as it passed the uniformed guards. It stopped in a "No Stopping" zone to let Sternbach out, walking stick first—to the nods and waves of passing people, greetings that linked several generations.

This ritual tells in a nutshell a story of love, success, and happiness, and also the story of the Sternbachs' ability to awaken admiration and affection among friends and acquaintances of all ages.

Sternbach has not been to his office since autumn 2002. He finds it difficult to walk; the stick no longer gives him proper support. What had troubled his wife for a long time now began to worry Sternbach too: the fear of falling and injuring himself. With the sensibility that the couple have always been able to rely on, Sternbach restricted his radius to their house and its immediate surroundings. Forever? For the time being! For with the sensibility comes hope that one will soon be able to do what one wants.

With characteristic intellectual strength and philosophical cheerfulness, Sternbach fashioned his lot in life into a program for living. The late 1950s is a particularly dramatic instance of this. Sternbach had gone his own route in the tranquilizer project in his research laboratory in Nutley, New Jersey, home of the U.S. affiliate of Roche, the Swiss-based healthcare company. As a result he lost his position in the official research group. Ignoring colleagues' condescension for the rebel who was on the wrong track, he doggedly pursued his ideas, developing the insights gained during research for his doctoral dissertation, to discover—at the moment that his patient manager finally reached the end of his tether—the first of the "minor tranquilizers." It was marketed in 1960 as Librium. Valium followed in 1963, sealing the phenomenal breakthrough in benzodiazepine research, and bringing Roche incredible financial success—billions of dollars over a period of many years.

Librium and Valium symbolize the achievements of a lifetime. As scientific answers, though, they do not mark the culmination of a life's work, but raise new questions that keep this field of research topical. Sternbach himself views his discovery not as a conclusion, but as a part of a continuation of the scientific exploration to be pursued by scientists of subsequent generations.

Esteem and Fame

In 1973, Sternbach retired from Roche with a pension that ensured his financial security. Since then he has worked as a consultant with his former company. His office is crammed full of books and files; Post-Its everywhere give some idea of the legendary chaos of his laboratory. Until well into his 94th year he sat down at his desk every day from Monday to Friday, pushed aside the piles of paper with his forearms, and edited his autobiographical notes. He read for a while in the library and ate lunch in the staff canteen. These are privileges—expressions of esteem, and a source of quiet pleasure—starting with the perfunctory security check and his stopping in a no-stopping zone. Even the young employees knew Dr. Sternbach, greet and stop to chat with him.

Fame embraced Sternbach warmly. Accolades gain special importance in the autumn of life—as irreplaceable as the "love and drive" from Monday to Friday for years beyond the diamond wedding anniversary.

Why did Sternbach become a discoverer, and why did he remain one? Why did he fight for his discoveries, working night after night in their cause? And why did he continue, despite the danger that the drugs that resulted from his research could be abused?

"To help the sick," says Sternbach, "not everybody, just those that suffer." He adds, "I was successful because I loved my work and was completely dedicated, like any true artist."

Sternbach has finally received the recognition he has always deserved. He knows it and appreciates it, with a modesty that far exceeds his pride. Even today he accepts any praise for his achievements as unwarranted: he, a great chemist prevented from studying chemistry through malice, hate, and inhuman madness.

Surmounting Suffering

Anti-Semitism in Poland colored Sternbach's experience and presented obstacles in his path. A realist, he accepted that Jewish students were effectively barred from the study of pharmacy or medicine. However, this acceptance in no way diminished his desire to succeed in the one subject he really loved—chemistry. With a mixture of prudence and conviction-driven stubbornness, he forged his own roundabout route; despite being Jewish, he was permitted to study pharmacy only because his father was a pharmacist, having established his profession in that field before it was denied to Jews. Then, with a pharmacy degree added to his name, Sternbach obtained permission to study chemistry.

Although fate and circumstance dictated hardship, he bore the difficulty with character—during the 1920s as a student in Krakow, in the years preceding his studies, as well as afterward. The scientific and private sections of Sternbach's biography—to the extent that one can separate them—play out along circuitous routes, detours, and narrow paths along the edge of a precipice.

Transcendent Lightness of Being

Hearing of such harassment and the need to repeatedly defend oneself in most unfavorable circumstances makes listeners angry. Yet, the Sternbachs' account of these experiences is free of accusation. They talk about their most bitter hours with matter-of-factness, even a laconic smile. This is when their philosophical cheerfulness comes into play. There are two sides to it. On the one hand, it is the cheerfulness and transcendent lightness that masters afflictions, prejudices, and existential difficulties supremely well; on the other hand it is the cheerfulness and transcendent lightness of refusing to let potential concerns about the future restrict their immediate freedom. Today is today and tomorrow is tomorrow.

It all began in Abbazia, in the twilight of the Austro-Hungarian empire, before World War I. It all began a long time ago, in another age, in a remote corner of Europe.

Chapter 2

Pearl of the Adriatic

Leo Henryk Sternbach, the elder child of a Polish Jew and his Hungarian Jewish wife, was born in Abbazia on the Istrian Peninsula on May 7, 1908. His brother Gyuszi, born 3 years later, died young of scarlet fever. The town, the Nice of the East and one of the most fashionable spas on the Adriatic coast, was part of the Austro-Hungarian Empire until after World War I. In 1920, it passed to Italy, and in 1947, as a result of World War II, to Yugoslavia. Now part of the independent republic of Croatia, which gained international recognition in 1992 and established its authority over the whole peninsula 6 years later, the "Pearl of the Adriatic," with its restored Art Nouveau hotels, has experienced a renaissance as the tourist center Opatija.

The communist dictatorship put an end to the former splendor that had been the reality for the Sternbachs. Once emperors and kings came to Abbazia for rest and recuperation, followed by fashionable society and the demimonde. James Joyce stayed there, as did the world boxing champion Primo Carnera, the tenor Beniamino Gigli, and the composers Gustav Mahler and Giacomo Puccini.

"Abbazia," wrote Henryk Sienkiewicz, a Polish Nobel prize winner and author of *Quo Vadis*, in a letter, "has everything: mountains, good air, it is well protected, and is on the sea with its healthy breezes." The Russian writer and playwright Anton Chekhov, however, complained that the hotels and their ugly petit bourgeois architecture destroyed the view of the bay.

Isadora Duncan, the American dancer, on the other hand, found the place inspiring, and recorded in her memoirs:

A palm growing below the window of our villa drew complete attention; it was the first time that I had seen a palm growing outdoors. Every day I observed how its beautiful leaves fluttered in the morning breeze, and from it I got that light quivering in the hands and fingers.

Thus, Abbazia appeared on stage, artistically sublimated in the gentlest of movements.

Father Sternbach's Business Sense

By moving from Krakow to the spa and bathing resort where cultured living was a way of life, the elder Sternbach revealed his view of personal happiness and good sense for business.

Sternbach wrote in his autobiographical notes:

My father was apparently not a very good student. Therefore, his parents had him study pharmacy, a study which at that time took only 3 years and needed only 6 years of high school. Thus, he began studying pharmacy in Lemberg (Lwow) at the age of 16. At the age of 19 he finished his studies and apparently became a master of pharmacy (magister pharmaciae) but had to practice a few years until he achieved the right to manage a pharmacy.

He worked for a few years in a pharmacy in Krakow (Magister Rosenberg's), which was then Austrian. He decided afterward to open a pharmacy in Abbazia, which was a flourishing spa on the Adriatic Sea, the only Austrian sea resort.

My mother's grandmother, who lived in Hungary, owned a villa in Abbazia. My mother spent her summer vacations with her parents in

*that villa and met my father. After a very short time they fell in love
and my father proposed. My mother was 17 and my father was 35.*

*My father came to Orosháza (a town near Szeged in Hungary) to
be introduced to the family, who were very upset that a member of
their clan would marry a Polish Jew, a member of the lowest class of
Jews. My father, however, must have succeeded in convincing them
that he was not so bad, and they got married in 1907.*

*As a result of this, I, Leo Henryk Sternbach, was born on May 7,
1908, to Michael Abraham Sternbach and Piroska "Piri" Sternbach-
Cohn in Abbazia.*

Medical Center

The natural beauty, the healthy climate, and the rapid growth in
tourism following the opening of the Southern Railway Company
(Südbahn-Gesellschaft) also attracted the sick and ailing to Abbazia,
and with them physicians. Theodor Billroth (1829–1894), a German sur-
geon, enhanced the town's reputation as a health resort. Julius Glax
(1846–1922), a Viennese scientist of bathing, organized a world congress
on thalassotherapy and treated prominent patients. By 1912 there were
12 clinics in the town, specializing in the treatment of bronchitis,
asthma, and heart disease. This environment also offered interesting
business prospects for pharmacists. The elder Sternbach acquired the
Kromir & Poriz pharmacy in the Mandria Bazar on the main street. He
ran a very successful enterprise, as inventor of ovolecithin-based Ovol
lozenges and Laurol, a dermatological treatment for rheumatism made
from laurel leaves.

It is quite possible that the older Sternbach passed on his talent for
invention to his son, in whom it blossomed into genius. At any rate, as
a child Leo Sternbach spent a lot of time in the pharmacy, helping his
father where he could—and unable to resist the temptation to help
himself to fruit gums, licorice, and sweet-tasting pills.

Ethnic Mix and Anti-Semitism

The immediate environs, too, had the feel of a paradise. Neighbors of the pharmacy included the souvenir shop of a Palestinian, Abu-Khalil, Kadish's musical instruments and sheet music, Köraus's glazier's shop, the Jewish butcher Hus, Tauber and Barbini's Italian restaurant, and the post office.

The city was an ethnic mix. The local Croatians, mostly farmers, fishermen, or hotel workers, were poor. Aside from Croatian Abbazia, there was a Polish, Hungarian, Czech, Slovak, Italian, and Jewish Abbazia as well. Since the end of the 19th century, Jewish businessmen, hoteliers, and doctors had played a leading role in the town. Jews built the first sanitariums. Initially, Jewish religious services were held in the Pension Breiner and later in the Pension Stern. The Jewish cemetery was laid out in 1912, and construction of the synagogue began in 1926.

The arrival of Jewish immigrants triggered a latent anti-Semitism that became overt in the 1930s, with Mussolini's proclamation of his "provisions to defend the Italian race." Leo Sternbach can recall Christian classmates in primary school calling him "dirt."

Family and Religion

The Sternbach family moved in upper middle class circles. They made no secret that they were Jewish, but were not very observant, although they did celebrate the High Holidays: Rosh Hashanah, the Jewish New Year, and Yom Kippur, the Day of Atonement. Leo's mother observed the rules of fasting, but his father did not. "People who work do not have to fast," explained his mother with a mixture of seriousness and ironic reproof. Leo Sternbach has never tried to hide the fact that he is a Jew, because "I was born a Jew," but he refuses to take part in any religious activity on the grounds that all religion is "senseless and negative"; nor does he believe in God. He married a Christian and his sons were brought up as Christians. But there was never any question of his rejecting Judaism or converting to Christianity, which he felt would have been a cowardly act.

His paternal grandparents ran a moving business, hauling cargo in horse-drawn carriages in Galicia. They had one daughter, Celina, and four sons. His father's oldest brother, Leon, became a professor of history, Greek, and Latin at the Jagiellonian University in Krakow; his brother Mieczyslaw was a senior railway official, and Edek, the youngest, was a lawyer. His maternal grandparents came from Hungary. His grandmother's first husband, the father of his mother Piri, was a Cohn; after her husband's death she married a divorced bank director, Manó Zsengery.

Because Sternbach's father did not speak Hungarian and his mother did not speak Polish, the family spoke German at home. Mother and son, however, conversed in Hungarian. The language of the town was Croatian. The young Sternbach's friends were, in the eyes of his disapproving mother, "rascals" of lower social standing.

Although his father loved Gyuszi, his younger son, more than the elder, Leo worshipped his father as understanding and "never reproachful"—unlike his mother, from whom he received a "very authoritarian and strict" upbringing.

The family lived in a rented apartment near the pharmacy, which Sternbach has vividly described in his autobiographical notes:

> *We lived on the third floor of a walk-up apartment building. Apartments were, at that time, rather primitive compared to the ones existing nowadays. We had a four-room apartment (rather small rooms) consisting of my parents' bedroom, our (Gyuszi's and mine) bed/playroom, a dining room and a drawing room ("Salon") which was used only when we had guests. We had only one toilet (WC), no bathroom. We washed in ceramic washbasins. The water (cold), we poured from a big pitcher standing next to it. Once a week we bathed in a public bathing establishment which had warm water. We had electric lights in every room except the kitchen, which was quite dark, since the only*

window opened on to the staircase. It was lit by a simple kerosene lamp. Refrigerators did not exist; we had an icebox which, on rare occasions, contained ice. Butter was kept in the summer under running water (from our pipes), which was quite cold, since it came from Monte Maggiore, 1,400 meters high. In winter we kept food between the double windows. We had double windows everywhere. In winter the rooms were heated by wood burning in Dutch-style tile stoves. For cooking we had in the kitchen an iron stove heated with wood (only wood was used). It also contained a water reservoir which yielded our warm water. No gas; for quick heating of small quantities, for instance my father's shaving water, we had a very simple alcohol burner. We had a maid who lived in a room in the attic.

Primary School

Leo Sternbach has two clear memories of September 1914: a first one that influenced his own life immediately, and a second that also affected him personally, but its fateful consequences would become apparent only much later.

The first memory is of his starting primary school, in a German-speaking class with two other Jewish children, in 1918. He was interested mainly in scientific subjects, in which there were only a few lessons a week, and later in Latin and French, but not in history. He produced excellent results without any effort, treated school exercises and homework as child's play, to the envy of his classmates, and gained his first experience as the target of anti-Semitic teasing and torments. He bore these with outward calm and inner bitterness, concluding that henceforth he would have to rely solely on himself and his own abilities. At an early age he learned that the best way to succeed and to prevail was by applying his sharp intelligence and intellectual zeal.

A minor incident characterizes Sternbach very well. He borrowed a book on the history of the coastal lands from his teacher to read at his leisure at home. One page seemed to him especially important. He tore it out, and was then afraid to return the damaged book. Sternbach has still not forgotten this incident. He recounts it with a smile, but would like nothing better than to return the history book and clear his conscience. This reflects his deeply rooted honesty. And the minor incident elucidates Sternbach's precocious ability to focus intensely on topics that he recognizes as important, even if they are not his personal preference. This diligence and uprightness are properties that would distinguish Sternbach as a researcher.

A World of Privation and Radical Change

Sternbach was 6 years old at the outbreak of the World War I and 10 at the end. He came through it unscathed; it was never a direct threat to his existence, but rather an event experienced through daily privations. As sales at the pharmacy declined, his father could no longer afford to employ an assistant, and his wife and elder son had to help out. For financial reasons, the household also had to do without the services of a maid. There were shortages of certain foodstuffs, such as sugar, flour, and butter. Instead of bread, the family often ate polenta sweetened with figs. New clothes were also scarce; Leo Sternbach wore a coat cut from military cloth.

Abbazia was untouched by the fighting. Occasionally a military airplane flew over the town. A bomb, dropped intentionally or unintentionally, caused some damage in the local woods. The town could hear the sound of cannon fire in the surrounding forests. The distant noise of the terrible battles at the Isonzo river drifted over Istria. But the destruction spared Abbazia. After the war, the city was occupied by Italians and incorporated into the province of Venezia Giulia.

Ten-year-old Leo Sternbach followed the historic turn of events with childlike delight—as a particularly keen and meticulous observer, which was later revealed in his natural interest in chemical processes. His autobiographical notes emphasize his joy in sensational effects, relegating to the background his recollection of a serious accident that could have severely injured his younger brother:

The Italian troops were very nice to us children. They played with us, gave us many rounds of carbine (rifle) shells, which we opened by inserting the top of the cartridge into a door-keyhole and bending it down until the upper part of the brass shell split. We emptied many shells, collected all the gun powder (nitrocellulose) on a big flat rock and burned it. It was consumed in a few seconds and gave a strong 2–4 feet high yellow flame. Under those conditions, it did not explode. We also discovered an outside storage place for ca. 1/2-inch diameter glass tubes and used these tubes for our purposes. We stuck about 7 inch long pieces into the ground, filled them with the nitrocellulose gunpowder—which was not powder at all, but consisted of about 3/8-inch long cylindrical bead-like pieces that looked like celluloid (diameter ca. 1/16 inch), like a lead in a pencil and set fire to it. The burning pieces of this "gunpowder" flew out of the tube and gave a cascade-like firework effect.

Friends of my parents saw us on one of the side streets playing with the shells and promptly reported it to my parents. This had very unpleasant repercussions. My mother ordered me to throw out immediately all the pretty brass shells which I had collected in my drawers. I put them all in a tin box which I had handy at home and buried them in the woods, quite near to our apartment, planning to retrieve them after the excitement had subsided. Unfortunately, however, when the time was right I could not find the box again. Somebody else could have unearthed my cache or I did not find the right place again.

The source of many interesting experiments was also provided by 'carbide', calcium carbide, which was used for the lights of the Italian motor trucks. This vile-smelling dark gray gravel-like material, about 1/2 inch in diameter, produced acetylene on contact with water, a gas that contained an impure phosphorus which smelled like garlic and burned with a very bright white flame. We stole it or got it from Italian soldiers and used it in the following manner. We punctured the flat undamaged end of a small used tin can (for canned beans, etc. about 3 inches in diameter and about 5 inches in height) and put this can over a few pieces of carbide which were moistened. Urine lent itself very well to this purpose. The acetylene formed, creating an explosive mixture with the air still present in the can. A burning match held to the tiny opening gave a nice explosion and the can was blown high into the air. If you did not remove your hand very quickly, the can hit you quite painfully.

An exciting and worrisome accident happened around 1921 when Gyuszi was racing an Italian car on the main street and ran full force into a truck coming in the opposite direction. He fell backwards to the ground and ended up under the camion, miraculously without being touched at all by the wheels. This happened in front of our pharmacy and he was brought to my father, who started to clean the blood from his swollen nose and face, realizing only after a while, that it was his own son whom he was treating. He was then brought to the hospital and we spent a very tense afternoon and night, until we were told that he had not suffered any major injuries. After coming home the next day, he stated nonchalantly that all he noticed was that it stank badly under the camion.

Beyond the children's unclouded everyday life, in which even accidents caused little more than a fright, radical changes were taking place. On October 29, 1918, the Croatian parliament declared the country's independence from Austro-Hungary. A month later, on December 1, 1918, Croatia, Serbia, and Slovenia united to form the Kingdom of Serbs, Croats, and Slovenes. The port cities of Rijeka and Zadar as well as the Istria peninsula—and thus Abbazia—were ceded to Italy.

The war and its consequences had finally reached the children. The Italian state insisted on Italian as the required language and closed the Austrian schools which taught in German. Neither Leo nor his brother

Gyuszi spoke Italian. Their parents and those of other children in the same situation got together and decided to employ German-speaking private teachers. This in turn meant that in June, at the end of the school year, the children had to take their examinations at an official educational institution before they could be promoted to the next class. The nearest examination center accessible by train was Villach, one hundred miles away in the Austrian province of Carinthia. The Sternbach children passed the examinations with mediocre results. This is not surprising, inasmuch as the series of modestly paid teachers, most of them Austrian, accepted the job in Abbazia primarily on account of the pleasant climate, and took a fairly relaxed attitude toward their pedagogical duties. One teacher suffered from tuberculosis and another was an alcoholic.

Move to Villach and Graz

Inevitably, Leo Sternbach's schooling suffered. Although he passed geography, mathematics, physics, and Latin, he failed history. With heavy hearts, his parents accepted the recommendation of the Latin master in Villach that their 13-year-old son move from Abbazia to Villach and enroll in the town's secondary school. The advantages of the newfound freedom soon outweighed his initial homesickness. The young Sternbach sensibly acquiesced to his parents' decision, found his feet as a pupil, and enthusiastically devoted his free time to chemistry experiments.

In the strongly Christian environment, however, he suffered increasingly from anti-Semitic bullying. This experience convinced his parents to remove their son from the school in Villach and place him in another one in Graz, one hundred miles to the east. The train connections between Abbazia and Graz were better, but that was the only advantage. Leo Sternbach found the anti-Semitism in the new school even worse than in the old. One of his teachers was an open and active supporter of Hitler, of Austria's union with Germany, and of a militaristic, nationalistic, and anti-Semitic Greater Germany. Moreover, the local rabbi compelled Sternbach, now 14 years old and living with a Jewish family, to attend religious instruction. This coerced public demonstration of his religious affiliation made it even more difficult for him to hold his own in an openly anti-Semitic environment. The only other Jewish pupil in his class was very Orthodox, which led him to keep his distance from Sternbach. It is indicative of his religious attitude that no matter how much he applied himself, he was unable to learn Hebrew. The fact that Graz and Montclair, New Jersey, where Sternbach has lived since 1941, are today twin cities, is for him one of history's bad jokes.

Starting Over Again

What oppressed their son in Graz also weighed on the parents. The separation, initially decided on as an educational godsend, was now a cause of great concern, one that was exacerbated by economic problems. The business of the once flourishing pharmacy was sluggish. For patriotic reasons, the parents had invested their wealth in war bonds and lost everything. The family faced serious questions about their future, partly triggered by the pressure on them from the Italian government to become Italian citizens. Sternbach's father, however, did not want this and chose another course. He decided to move the family to the newly independent Poland, where he had two brothers, and to take up citizenship there. They settled in Krakow, with its splendid Gothic and Renaissance architecture, where the older Sternbach's two brothers lived: Leon, the university professor, and Edek, the lawyer.

Despite the support of the family, the new beginning was full of hardship. The family found a first-floor flat in a new apartment block in the Kazimierz district, the Jewish ghetto, where the elder Sternbach was able to open a pharmacy after overcoming many bureaucratic hurdles. But it took quite some time before matters reached this stage.

Leo Sternbach first had to learn Polish, a language he did not know at all. He spoke German and Hungarian fluently, the former because it was the family's common language and the latter because it was the language he used with his mother. From his reserved and taciturn father, on the other hand, he had not learned any Polish. Because his parents felt it was necessary to remain in Abbazia for another year or two to settle their complicated and somewhat uncertain business affairs, they sent their son ahead to Poland on his own.

His destination was Bielsko-Biala in Silesia in southern Poland, which had a secondary school at which German was the language used; in addition to the normal curriculum, Sternbach also had to cram to learn Polish; he had a linguistic ration of 20 new words a day.

Sternbach found accommodation first with the family of Julius Werner, a Jewish teacher at the secondary school, and later with a Jewish widow, Mrs. Fischer. He made friends with her daughter Martha, enjoyed the visits of her classmates, and cast the friendliest glances at Grete Weiner.

Sternbach liked it in Bielsko-Biala. There was less anti-Semitism than in Villach and Graz. He felt at ease in his class, where half the pupils were Jewish. He received good grades in mathematics, German, Latin, French, and English, but he still had trouble with history, and he regretted that so little time was devoted to scientific subjects. He saw his parents in Abbazia during summer vacations and over the High Holidays. He planned the train journeys so that he could visit his uncles and cousins in Krakow and his grandmother in Budapest.

Graduation and Decision to Settle in Poland

In 1926, at the age of 18, Leo Sternbach graduated from secondary school. From his perspective, passing his university entrance examinations had been a difficult challenge, and he felt that he had been only moderately successful. But we may take a different view. To achieve his university entrance, Sternbach's route had taken him through two languages (German and Polish), four countries (Austro-Hungarian Croatia, Italian Croatia, Austria, and Poland), anti-Semitism, and the separation from his parents. Without deep intelligence, a strong will, and drive, it is unlikely he would have gotten through secondary school, let alone the final examinations. His inner straight and narrow path kept the upper hand against the threatening external detours. Sternbach revealed for the first time his ability to focus all his attention on achieving a goal that he had set himself. By passing the university entrance examination he had also demonstrated that he had the ability to meet the challenges of life.

That year, 1926, was also the year when the family finally settled in Poland. At any rate, it was as final as any subsequent decisions; what at the time appeared to be permanent, was, in hindsight, only temporary. In summer 1926 Sternbach's parents moved from Abbazia to Krakow, where, after a long delay, his father received permission to open a pharmacy. That was shortly after Marshall József Pilsudski's putsch, which put an end to the frequent changes of government in Poland.

Leaving Abbazia did not mean that the family had more favorable prospects. It only meant that they had exchanged a grim uncertainty for a less grim uncertainty. Or to put it another way, the choice was between an environment ruled by the unpopular Italians, which offered no future, or Poland, the elder Sternbach's homeland, which offered a glimmer of hope. The elder son passed the university entrance examination, the key to a scientific education, which did mean that one important door was opened. But 1926 also cast an unexpected shadow over the family. In the fall, Gyuszi, Sternbach's younger brother, caught scarlet fever. At that time, the disease was usually fatal, even for people who received the best medical treatment. In this case fate was not prepared to make an exception: Gyuszi died at the age of 15 on November 16.

There was another respect in which 1926 was significant, this time in an optimistic, permanently cheerful, indeed happy way. Leo Sternbach made friends with his cousin Ludwik. The conspicuously red-haired son of his Uncle Edek and Aunt Klara became his enthusiastic partner first in table tennis and then at cards. After first playing tarot, Sternbach discovered bridge, which he took up enthusiastically and which has remained a real passion to this day. Sternbach loves bridge, indeed all games of chance. He was and is extremely good at them. He loves to play games of fortune and finds them a source of great pleasure and relaxation. His true love, however, was and always will be chemistry. And so he continued on the path to his destiny.

The Lure of Chemistry

Finally, in fall 1926 Sternbach enrolled at the university. As the son of a pharmacist he was accepted for the study of pharmacy without any difficulty. That was the course his father wanted him to take, because it would enable the younger Sternbach to help with and eventually take over the family business. But Leo Sternbach still dreamed of chemistry.

What Rainer Maria Rilke wrote to a young poet applied equally to the young Sternbach and chemistry:

> *Think it over carefully. Determine the reason that drives you to write; examine, whether you can feel it in your heart of hearts, do you feel that you would have to die if you were forbidden to write? Above all: do you ask yourself in the dead of night: do I have to write? Search for an answer in the depths of your heart. And if you answer in the affirmative, if you should respond to this serious question with a strong, simple "I must," then build your life around this necessity. Your life, even at its most trivial and negligible, must symbolize and bear witness to this urge.*

For Sternbach, the "strong and simple" answer was "Yes, I must be a chemist!" The study of pharmacy helped pave the way to that goal. He completed his pharmacy degree within 3 years, acquiring an extensive knowledge of botany and learning how to make extracts, infusions, and tinctures from leaves, roots, and bark. He slaved away making up prescriptions. In 1929 he was awarded a master's degree in pharmacy: magister pharmaciae.

The Reward for Perseverance

Doggedly persevering through his training as a pharmacist, Sternbach used that background as a stepping stone. He then continued his studies, this time in the field of organic chemistry under Professor Karol Dziewoński, who supervised Sternbach's successful doctoral thesis in 1931, and who subsequently found Sternbach a position as a research assistant and lecturer. Growing anti-Semitism within the University of Krakow was exploited with the aim of filling the desirable post held by the Jew Sternbach with a Polish Christian. Dziewoński resisted until the end of 1936, and then smoothed the way for Sternbach to apply for a scholarship financed by Feliks Wiślicki, a Jewish textile magnate.

Going West

Under the scholarship, Sternbach received a monthly stipend of 300 zloties, which was a handsome amount at the time. It enabled Sternbach to kill two birds with one stone: to escape from Poland and the pressures of anti-Semitism, and to pursue his scientific career in chemistry. The former proved to be illusory; the latter, however, turned out to be a rewarding opportunity, although initially only partially. His path led to Vienna, where Sternbach arrived on March 1, 1937, at the age of 29.

He had become a pharmacist and then with perseverance and passion he trained as a highly gifted chemist. He had enormous drive, had modest material needs, made friends easily and was known for his social graces and humor. He openly professed his Judaism, but he was not religious. He was fluent in German, Hungarian, and Polish. Having first emigrated eastward from Croatia to Poland, he now reversed direction, with Vienna as his first stop on his westward journey. At the time, Sternbach could not know that this first stop would not be his last. He did not plan the course of his biography. He wanted to live for and with chemistry. He was looking for the most favorable external conditions in which to fulfill his desire. He was not to know that the circumstances that he had identified as favorable would not always be so.

He was now in Vienna, full of hope and dreams of the scientific and research challenges ahead of him. In his own mind, he had no doubts. However, the strength to shape his own life would prove to be weaker than the influence of providence and fate.

Chapter 3

First Blossoming

Disappointment in Vienna

The Wiślicki Scholarship opened doors. It testified to the holder's scientific competence, and, no less important, it testified to the holder's economic independence. Anybody could offer Sternbach a position in the knowledge that this would not incur a financial burden. Wolfgang Pauli, professor for medicinal colloid chemistry, had probably taken all these considerations into account when he responded in the affirmative to Sternbach's inquiry about a position at the "Little Red Chemical Institute" in Vienna's Währingerstrasse.

Gisela Kerber, a friend of Sternbach's mother, and her husband, a freemason like Sternbach's father, helped him to find very plain, cheap accommodations. Sternbach would have been better off had he not looked for more comfortable lodgings on his own; the room he found a few days later had bedbugs. It was a miserable start to life in Vienna. It was also a bad omen.

Aside from colloidal chemistry with Wolfgang Pauli, Sternbach also wanted to work in organic chemistry. He went knocking at the door of Professor Sigmund Fränkel, an acquaintance of one of his aunts, who offered him a place in his private laboratory for medicinal chemistry. The laboratory specialized in the synthesis of quinine, whose structure had at that time not yet been determined. However, from the start he found the working conditions unacceptable. The laboratory was freezing cold, the equipment dirty, and the assistant unqualified.

Sternbach soon gave notice, and asked Professor Ernst Späth, head of the Second Chemical Institute of the University of Vienna, if he could work with him in a full- or part-time position. The reply was negative; Späth did not accept Jews as co-workers. In Vienna, the Wiślicki Scholarship opened doors only a crack, if at all. Anti-Semitism had caught up with Sternbach again.

One of His Most Important Decisions

April 27, 1937, was a turning point that would have far-reaching consequences for the life of the young scientist. On that day, Leopold Ruzicka, the famous professor of chemistry at the Federal Institute of Technology (ETH) in Zurich, and Nobel prize winner in 1939, held a lecture at the Chemistry and Physics Society in Vienna titled "On the Male Sexual Hormone." Sternbach was in the audience that gathered to hear the talk in the large lecture theater at Strudlhofgasse 4. It was another irony of history that Späth presided over the evening's events.

The lecture galvanized Sternbach. He wrote a letter to Ruzicka, asking whether he could work in his institute at the ETH. Ruzicka's consent came almost immediately. In this case, the Wiślicki Scholarship demonstrated its influence. Moreover, Ruzicka, like Sternbach, had been born in Croatia, on September 13, 1887, in Vukovar, where he was brought up a Catholic. He was known for helping young Jewish scientists from Eastern Europe. On October 1, 1937, Sternbach arrived in Zurich.

He describes this in his autobiographical notes:

After stopping at a hotel near the train station, I went immediately to the chemistry building of the ETH (Federal Institute of Technology) to see Prof. Ruzicka. I was met by his right-hand privatdozent (approximately an associate professor) Dr. M.W. Goldberg, who greeted me very cordially and told me that he was to take care of me, as Prof. Ruzicka was away for a few days. He showed me the laboratory bench which was assigned to me and introduced me to the assis-

*tant, Dr. Klaus Hoffman (2 years older than I), who was in charge of
the laboratory, which housed about 15 scientists. He is now a professor or professor emeritus at the University of Pittsburgh. He proposed
that I first look for a room to live in and suggested a Mrs. Kreuzer,
who had an apartment at Universitätsstrasse 87, quite near the Chemical Institute. I went there and was able to get a very nice room with
a view of the town and the Uetliberg on the other side. This proved
to be one of the most important decisions and formed my whole future
life. There I met her daughter, Herta Kreuzer, whom I married in
1940 and who is still my wife and the mother of our two boys.*

This plain, succinct account covers Sternbach's first two and a half
years in Zurich. The commentary, "This proved to be one of the most
important decisions and formed my whole future life," reads like a sudden rush of emotion in the otherwise extremely rational prose. Or to
put it another way: Sternbach is rigorous in his objectivity. In writing
about private matters he exercises great detachment. He appears to be
observing himself, as it were, employing almost the same objectivity he
learned as a chemist: he jots down notes about his own person in such
a cool tone that he could be writing about a stranger.

But appearances can be deceiving. In direct contact not only is
Sternbach likeable and friendly, but he also radiates a genuine warm-
heartedness. He is very open in his approach to people. The detached
account of his own experiences is simply a reflection of the fact that
he is not full of his own importance. This is modesty in practice, coupled with Sternbach's conviction that all that matters is reality, not
appearances.

For Sternbach, what counts was and is how he was received when it
did count, whether he received a warm or a cold welcome. The remark
"Goldberg greeted me very cordially" must be understood in this context. If Sternbach had not been received so warmly, he would have felt
uneasy at the ETH from the very beginning. He expected respect. The
lack of respect was hurtful. For in one regard he was anything but modest: his awareness of his ability as a chemist. He knew what he was

worth. He knew that he already had done excellent work, and knew he had the potential for outstanding achievements in the future.

The statement that marrying Herta Kreuzer was one of his most important decisions is, of course, absolutely true. It is a happy marriage. Herta is the partner that takes care of everything for her husband so that he can pursue his career commitments and private interests unhindered. She is his support in good times and bad. Sternbach discusses every important decision in detail with his wife. She is the only person whom he trusts implicitly. He acts on her advice. Anybody meeting Herta and Leo Sternbach notices that they love each other, are harmonious companions, and yet remain distinct personalities.

Herta Kreuzer-Sternbach

When they married in 1940, Herta Kreuzer was 20 years young, i.e., 12 years younger than Leo Sternbach. She grew up with her younger brother Konradin, who lives in Flüh, Canton of Solothurn, Switzerland, and her sister Silvia, who died in the fall of 2001. Her parents, Maria Diem-Kreuzer and Otto Kreuzer, were divorced in 1929, and her mother received custody of the children. Despite their restricted circumstances, Mrs. Kreuzer set great store by elegant appearances. By day she worked as a sales assistant in a silk company, at night she sewed blouses. Letting rooms brought in extra income. Herta was responsible for the household, and earned some pocket money on the side by delivering flowers for the florist on the ground floor of their apartment block at Universitätsstrasse 87.

She completed a commercial apprenticeship at Emelka, a firm of film distributors in Zurich, although she does not have particularly happy recollections of this period, least of all of her boss. She then worked as an office worker in a raincoat factory, and after that for Leutert, butchers in the Schützengasse, in the middle of downtown Zurich.

It took a lot of love and quite of bit of courage for a Christian to marry a Jew during World War II. The threat of invasion by national socialist Germany hung over Switzerland, and Zurich itself was not free of latent anti-Semitism. To marry in Zurich, the young couple had to pay a substantial fee of 2,000 Swiss francs, the equivalent of almost $1,500 at the time, which served as a preliminary down payment for any welfare payments that the young couple might have claimed in the event that they were unable to support themselves. The Sternbachs did not have that much money. Therefore, they married in a registry office in Basel, which did not levy any fee, and, to please Mrs. Kreuzer, also went through a church ceremony in Zurich, for which no fee was required, either.

By marrying Leo Sternbach, Herta Sternbach lost her Swiss citizenship and acquired her husband's Polish nationality. A few days after the wedding, she received a communication from the Alien Police saying that, as she was now a "tolerated foreigner," she had to leave Switzerland as soon as possible. That was the usual practice at the time.

Today the Sternbachs talk about this harsh treatment without rancor, even with a smile. But this in no way mitigates the outrageousness of the procedure. While the record shows that the Swiss army and numerous Swiss citizens helped many refugees during that tragic period in history, the Swiss attitude that the boat was full was a hard-hearted one that ultimately relented under the weight of intense historical scrutiny and critical public opinion.

Working at the ETH

Sternbach was happy with his work at the ETH, because, as he puts it, he was given the interesting challenge of establishing the position of the double bonds of abietic and dextropimaric acids.

Professor Ruzicka had 15 scientists in his laboratory, an international group from Switzerland, Germany, the Netherlands, Hungary, Croatia, Japan, and the United States. Sternbach got on very well with his superior and was friendly with some of his colleagues, among them Géza Müller from Trieste, who later settled in

Argentina; Cyril Grob, later professor of organic chemistry at the University of Basel; George Rosenkranz, a gifted bridge player who made a fortune as the inventor of cortisone compounds and emigrated first to Cuba and afterward to Mexico; Oskar Jeger; and Dr. Palma, the son of Sternbach's mother's dentist in Fiume/Rijeka. Sternbach supervised Jeger's diploma thesis, and Jeger went on to become a professor at the ETH.

Skiing, Mountain Climbing, Recreation

Another reason for the happy memories was Zurich's location as an ideal starting point for skiing and mountain climbing. To afford the pleasures of recreational excursions, Sternbach had to keep himself on a very tight budget. Even with the Wiślicki Scholarship he could not exactly live it up. He always walked from his room to the laboratory to save the 20-centimes tram fare. For lunch, he selected the cheapest choice in the student union and in the evening ate bread, butter, cheese, and occasionally cold cuts, in his room. Skiing and mountain climbing quite literally meant getting to the top under his own power; although ski lifts and mountain railways existed, they were prohibitively expensive. He had enough money only for the train journey from Zurich to Davos, Arosa, Engelberg, or the Flumser Mountains. He bought his provisions beforehand and carried them in his rucksack. When he spent the night in a mountain hut, he slept on straw.

Sternbach returned from these excursions, which usually began at midday on Saturday and ended on Sunday evening, satisfied by the experience of nature, strengthened by the physical activity, and stimulated by the lively company he went with:

One excursion, my "biggest feat," was a trip which was arranged every Easter by the Swiss railroad: by train and cog rail up to the Jungfraujoch, a night spent up there in the hut, then the next day a climb of the Lauberhorn, and back again to Jungfraujoch. The third morning (early) again down to Concordia Platz on hard, frozen snow, then up (about a 3-hour climb) to the Lötschenlücke, and a beautiful run (soft spring conditions on sun-exposed meadows) down to Goppenstein in the Wallis. The night spent in the hut was not very comfortable, altitude sickness, a headache, a thoroughly burnt face, blisters all over. I was not even quite sure that I would be able to make it down on skis and was afraid I might have to take the train back, but I somehow managed. The weather was magnificent and the whole excursion was a great success.

He divided the 3-week summer break between Switzerland and Poland. He visited his parents for the last time at Easter in 1939, 6 months before the Germans invaded his homeland.

What was not already part of his recreational activities would not become part of leisure interests later. Sternbach was never particularly interested in classical literature or classical music, museums, theater, or movies. His enthusiasms focused on nature and his scientific pursuits. Between them, these kept him fully occupied and provided the stimulation he needed. He never developed a strong interest in cultural matters. Bridge fascinated him. This card game played (and still plays) a leading role in his free time—his "sacred" evenings in the company of friends.

Dark Shadows of World War II

The late summer of 1939 caused Sternbach weeks of uncertainty and worry, even despondency. The shadows cast by World War II affected him, too. The German invasion of Poland on September 1, 1939, and the rapid advance of the German army meant the loss of his country of citizenship, on the one hand, and anxiety about the fate of his parents on the other. Sternbach learned from a Palestinian radio station that his father and mother were alive, a fact subsequently confirmed by postcards from Catholic acquaintances and eventually from his parents.

With each sign of life, his father's signature grew shakier, until finally it became illegible. The heavy smoker died of lung cancer on his 70th birthday—January 20, 1940. Catholic friends in Krakow hid his mother for the duration of the persecution of the Jews; in 1945, after the end of the war, her son was able to bring her to Switzerland.

Temporary Reprieve in Zurich and Prospects in Basel

In Switzerland, Sternbach was spared the anti-Semitism he had encountered in Krakow and Vienna. This was thanks, on the one hand, to the resolutely protective stance adopted by Professor Ruzicka and, on the other, to the willingness of Roche, the Basel-based chemical and pharmaceutical company, to employ Jews and protect their careers. This policy was supported by the company's management and, in particular, by Emil Christoph Barell, the chairman of the Board of Directors, who was married to a woman of Jewish origin.

Sternbach experienced fewer racially motivated difficulties at the ETH in Zurich than in Krakow and Vienna, both privately and professionally. But the ETH was not free of anti-Jewish hostility. The rabble-rousing attacks bounced off Professor Ruzicka. He did whatever he could to encourage his Jewish colleagues. However, this could not prevent questions about how long and in what function Sternbach could continue to work at the ETH. The final extension of the Wiślicki Scholarship, which had guaranteed an almost miraculous degree of independence, expired in March 1939. Ruzicka made Sternbach's continued employment dependent on support from the Rockefeller Foundation. Fortunately, it materialized, allowing Ruzicka to retain his postgraduate assistant in his laboratory on a salary of 350 Swiss francs a month, 50 francs more than the Wiślicki Scholarship had provided.

This reprieve was only temporary inasmuch as Sternbach knew that the ETH was not a permanent source of research and income for him. But it was long enough to experience a stroke of good fortune. Sternbach learned that Hoffmann-La Roche was looking for a research chemist. He applied, and was invited for a job interview with Chairman

Emil Christoph Barell and Markus Guggenheim, the director of research. On May 7, 1940, his 32nd birthday, he was offered the post. It was to be a unique and happy association for both sides, one that lasted for decades. And for Sternbach, it turned out to be more than a wise career choice; it was also a twist of fate that would prove to be vital to his existence. For not only did Roche, contrary to many other companies, employ Jews, but Roche would ultimately protect Sternbach and other endangered colleagues in the most perilous of circumstances.

Sternbach began working in Basel on June 1, 1940. He received a salary of 600 Swiss francs a month, well above a research chemist's starting salary. He rented a room with a bath in the Dufourstrasse, close to the Wettstein Bridge, and walked half an hour to work in the morning and back again in the evening.

Looking back, Sternbach recalls:

Since Roche had at that time started to work on a technical synthesis of riboflavin vitamin B_2, I was assigned one of the steps of this synthesis, the preparation of ribonolactone from arabonic acid. Glucose was used as starting material. It was oxidized to gluconic acid, arabonic acid, etc. One carbon atom was removed by oxidation. This ribonolactone was then used by another chemist, who worked on the next step of the synthesis.

These were interesting people who met on joining Roche, a good sprinkling of foreigners; the Swiss were almost in the minority. They included Dr. Hans Heinz Wüest, a technical director apparently of German origin; Dr. John J. Aeschlimann, of Bernese extraction, who grew up in England; Dr. Robert Duschinsky, a Viennese who was transferred by Roche from France to the United States, and who had a Jewish father and a Christian mother. Duschinsky invented and synthesized fluorouracil (a cancer drug) and submitted it for testing after the biochemist Charlie Heidelberger suggested to him that it might be an antimetabolite, an anticancer agent. I also met Dr. Walter Karrer, the brother of the well-known Zürich University Professor Paul Karrer, Dr. Warnat, a very left-oriented Sudeten-German, who wrote

his German notebooks in Cyrillic letters, since he was afraid that some-
body might steal his ideas, Dr. Klingenfuss, a German Nazi, the only
person who had longer conversations with me, since the Swiss in their
usual reserved way did not exude friendliness. The whole group was
under the direction of Dr. Ernst Preiswerk, a more down-to-earth
member of an old patrician Basel family. My first lab assistant and
co-worker was the 16-year-old Karl Hürlimann, who still corresponds
with me, sending me every year letters with sets of the first day issues
of "Pro Patria" and "Pro Juventute" stamps. We had very strict printed
rules and were not supposed to enter other laboratories than our own
without any special reasons.

On the same day I joined Roche, another chemist was also engaged.
This was Dr. Andreas Grüssner, a Hungarian, who was in a situa-
tion very similar to mine, since Hungary was also overrun by the
Germans. He was working with Prof. Reichstein in Basel, with whom
he had synthesized ascorbic acid (vitamin C). Dr. Grüssner and Dr.
Winterstein were two Roche people I had closer contact with. On some
Sundays we played monopoly in Dr. Winterstein's apartment, a game
he had obtained in or from Denmark. Most Sundays, however, I spent
in Zurich visiting Herta Kreuzer. With Grüssner, who was about my
age, I maintained a fairly close contact. At one time, I mentioned dur-
ing a conversation, that my monthly salary was Sfr. 650, assuming that
his would be the same. This caused considerable unpleasantness since
his salary was Sfr. 600, and he did not hesitate to complain to his supe-
riors about this discrepancy. This was corrected and I was consequently
very strictly advised not to discuss salaries with anybody!

Not long after Sternbach started working in Basel, Chairman Barell
of Roche informed him that the company intended to transfer him to
the chemical research facility that was to be established at Nutley, New
Jersey, in the United States. Sternbach told Barrell that if Roche wanted
to send him to America, they would have to be prepared to pay for a
trip for two, since he planned to marry Herta Kreuzer before leaving.
Barrell agreed and the newlyweds set sail for the New World.

Chapter 4

A Chemist of World Renown

Changes Caused by War

In 1941 Hitler invaded Yugoslavia, Greece, the Soviet Union, and North Africa. Japan attacked the United States, and in support the Axis powers, Germany and Italy, declared war on America, too.

Neutral Switzerland found itself in a precarious situation, surrounded as it was by the Axis powers. It was unclear whether Germany would invade, and if so, when. As food shortages became commonplace and economic pressures on the country increased, Switzerland mobilized amid growing tension between those in favor of resistance and those in favor of appeasement.

"Finally, on 21 May, after German tanks had reached the English Channel, and with the collapse of Belgium and France just a matter of time," Barell made the momentous decision to move the headquarters of Roche from Basel to the United States, before himself traveling to New York and on to Nutley, New Jersey. Hans Conrad Peyer's history of Roche continues:

Given the company's systematic efforts to shift operations westwards from 1936–1938 on, Barell's decision was no doubt a logical step. But the timing was unfortunate. In the eyes of those who had to stay behind, the chairman's departure could easily be construed as flight.

In autumn 1940 and the course of 1941, [Barell] had a number of the best people in Basel join him in Nutley. Ritz, head of publicity and chairman of the management committee in Basel, and René Janin, a French diplomat who had recently joined Roche, were given the task of building up an export department for the Western world. Its task was to ensure for the duration of the war that offices which did not have their own production facilities and could no longer be supplied from Basel would still receive supplies of Roche products. Similarly, Wüest, an expert in research and production, was brought over to establish research facilities and expand pharmaceutical production in Nutley, assisted by excellent chemists from Basel, including Aeschlimann, Lindenmaier, Hoffer, Wenner, Sternbach and Furter. In this way, Barell hoped to turn the extremely autonomous subsidiary in Nutley, which before the war was already manufacturing almost all Roche products itself, into the company's wartime headquarters with its own research facilities. Indeed, it did become one of the principal suppliers of vitamins to the United States and its allies. . . . [Henceforth,] research in Nutley produced a number of significant successes, including Gantrisin, in the two years from 1940 to 1942, employment at Nutley doubled from 669 to 1366, reaching 2000 by the end of the war in 1945, whereas in Basel it rose from 800 in 1940 to just 1200 in 1945. Starting in 1942, two large factories and a laboratory building were erected at Nutley to Salvisberg's plans.

Roche's operations on both sides of the Atlantic prospered. "With the departure of so many good research chemists for the United States," the Peyer history notes, "rumor had it that Roche was stopping all research in Basel. But . . . the remaining research group, revitalized with fresh, young talent, overcame the loss surprisingly well."

These political, economic, and corporate developments formed the backdrop to Sternbach's start in the United States. In addition, America also offered him a greater measure of personal safety.

Bureaucratic Hurdles and Atlantic Dangers

Herta Sternbach looked forward to the United States and the opportunities it offered her husband. However, she was deeply concerned about leaving her mother behind. Not only were the two women very close, but Herta Sternbach also helped to support her mother financially. Contrary to her expectations, her mother quickly came to terms with what was likely to be a long separation.

The travel preparations were difficult, and Roche gave the young couple help in every way it could. The visa was issued on the grounds that Sternbach was a specialist in the synthesis of vitamins and, hence, indispensable to the war effort. Both also met the requirements of the immigration quota, Herta Sternbach because she was Swiss-born and Leo Sternbach because he was classified as an Italian-born Austrian—Croatian Abbazia had been awarded to Italy after World War I.

The only feasible route to the United States was the Atlantic crossing in a Portuguese ship sailing from neutral Portugal. To this end, the Sternbachs were given so-called Swiss aliens' passports. These documents were valid for 3 months, did not mention the holder's nationality or religion, and could be used only for the purpose of emigration. Buying tickets proved to be tricky. To do so one had to have a Portuguese visa. But to get a Portuguese visa you had to provide proof of a ticket for the passage to the United States. A 50-dollar bill discreetly left at the right Portuguese counter at the right moment solved the problem.

Traveling through occupied France was not without risk. The Swiss authorities had to provide the German authorities with a list of emigrants for their approval. The Sternbachs set off from Geneva, where Mrs. Kreuzer had accompanied her daughter and son-in-law. They traveled in sealed railway cars to the Franco-Spanish border, took a bus for Barcelona at Port-Bou the next morning, and from there they took a train to Madrid. To enable the couple to recover from the strenuous trip, which included an unscheduled stop with a flat tire in the freezing mountain air in the Pyrenees, the Spanish subsidiary of Roche reserved a room for them at the Ritz. The next day they caught a train to Lisbon and, after waiting for a few days, boarded the *Serpa Pinto* on June 12, 1941. It was uncertain whether they would ever dock safely in Jersey City. Although the ship sailed under the flag of Portugal, a neutral country, on the open sea it was an easy target for German fighter bombers or submarines.

Although designed for 400 passengers, the *Serpa Pinto* was carrying 700, including a great number of non-Jewish Poles. On boarding, Herta Sternbach found that the single cabin she had reserved was not available. But she was able to travel in a first-class, three-bed cabin with hot and cold running water on Deck B and enjoyed the modest comfort. Leo Sternbach had initially reserved an uncomfortable third-class cabin, but for $163 was able to move to a four-bed cabin in first class.

During the day the Sternbachs lounged about in the deck chairs they had bought in Lisbon. Superb weather and a calm sea lent the trip a holiday atmosphere. Herta was never seasick, though Leo suffered from mild attacks. Lunch and dinner followed by dancing to a five-piece band provided a little entertainment and glamour to break the monotony of the uneventful days. Because the seven-course meals—hors d'oeuvres, soup, fish, meat, salad, and vegetables—were for the most part poorly prepared, for the Sternbachs the culinary highlight of the meal was always dessert. After pudding and cake they enjoyed strawberries, cherries, pears, bananas, oranges and, in particular, pineapple. One of the few attractions, at least for the women, was the possibility of having their fingernails painted red. Herta was one of a minority that chose not to follow this fashion.

Slow Journey

The Sternbachs had to while away 11 days on the high seas. The transition from the Old to the New World was a gradual process. In those days there were few flights, and even these ceased at the outbreak of war. The Sternbachs' slow passage suited their situation. They were relocating not only geographically, but, as Europeans, were also on the way to their new selves as future Americans. It was also an inner journey. And a journey of this nature takes much longer than the physical transportation. The ship's passage symbolized this transition, and may well have facilitated it. The shared experience of mastering the practical difficulties of emigration brought them closer together and gave them the strength to cope with the practical difficulties they would soon encounter on arrival.

After German, Hungarian, and Polish, Leo Sternbach was traveling to his fourth language, American English. It was another step in his progress westward. Europeans who went eastward at that time had a harder lot: they ended up under the advancing Communists. As a Jew, Sternbach had experienced anti-Semitism, which had been rampant in the East much earlier than in the West. He lived with and suffered under it on his path eastward from Croatia to Poland. In contrast, Europeans who were able to go westward at least had a chance of finding private happiness and professional success.

On June 22, 1941, the day on which Germany invaded the Soviet Union, the *Serpa Pinto* docked in Jersey City after a calm Atlantic crossing. It was very hot and very humid. A porters' strike delayed disembarkation. Wilhelm Wenner and Heinz Moritz Wüest welcomed the Sternbachs on behalf of Roche's chairman, Barell, and accompanied them in the company bus to the Marlboro Inn in Upper Montclair, New Jersey, where they were to stay for the next 2 weeks.

In her numerous letters to her mother, Herta Sternbach described it as a "wonderful, small hotel with a garden" and noted the "nice room and bath." "After the very beautiful trip" it suited her perfectly, and she was charmed by the greenness, trees, flowers, and small villas, but it was "terribly hot in this place."

A Different World

The Sternbachs knew, of course, that the United States would be "different" from Switzerland and the rest of Europe. They were prepared, for instance, for the new language, were able to make themselves understood without difficulty from the start, and quickly learned to make telephone calls in the new foreign language. However, they had not expected that they would have to buy a car. Private cars were still very much the exception in Switzerland, and in Europe in general, and were widely regarded as a sign of wealth. Surprised though they were by the role of the automobile in everyday life, the Sternbachs immediately realized that given the lack of public transportation they would be lost without a car. It would have taken Herta hours to do her shopping, and Leo even longer to get from Upper Montclair to the laboratory in Nutley. Although his colleagues offered to drive him to work, this was not a permanent solution.

At the end of June, they started taking driving lessons from one of the truck drivers at Roche, and shortly afterward bought a new light-gray four-seater Chevrolet. Because of restrictions owing to the war effort, it was not easy to buy a car, and theirs cost them $847. This was almost the entire amount that Roche had given the couple for furnishings. It put an end to their dream of new furniture and their own home. Their tight budget forced them to look for a furnished house to rent. They found one at 100 Buckingham Road, Upper Montclair, 10 minutes by car from the laboratory, with a garden and garage. They furnished it to suit their needs and tastes as best they could, and put the kitsch that the owner had left behind in the basement. They felt very grand in their sitting room with its English hearth, glass-enclosed porch, dining room, two bedrooms, and a bathroom. Still very European, the Sternbachs were amazed by the comfort of the kitchen, with its breakfast nook by the refrigerator, washing machine, and vacuum cleaner, which Leo, too, eagerly tried out. Their monthly rent, including gas, heating and utilities, came to $60. The new arrivals now had the basics.

One week after their arrival they found time for their first visit to New York, which was half an hour away by car. They made the best of what they had. Only the heat and humidity caused them problems. They did not complain about the lack of money; indeed, they regularly sent money to their mothers. They saw the positive side of things. Leo Sternbach wrote with delight to his mother-in-law on June 26, 1941, that "all the necessities of life, particularly food, are incredibly cheap." And on July 11: "I believe that we will be happy here."

Sternbach's supervisors, colleagues, and their wives contributed to this feeling. They helped out with hints, furniture and household appliances. The narrower circle, whose advice and support helped them settle in and laid the foundations of friendship, included Werner Lindenmaier, head of vitamins, and his Russian wife Bronja; Albert Frey, head of production, and his wife Lilly; and Hans Ritz, head of finance, and his wife Gertrud. Barell, the big boss, invited the Sternbachs to dinner and the theater in New York a number of times, as he did with other Roche Ph.D.s.

Teething Problems in the Laboratory

Toward the end of June, Sternbach started working on his research, "slowly," as he noted in a letter to his mother-in-law. Sternbach recalls:

At Roche I was housed with the other chemists, who were brought over from Switzerland around the same time, in a new 1-story plant building, building 25. There were 6 long benches and 2 large hoods in the huge laboratory. Dr. Hoffer and Dr. Wenner were already in. I was the third one to arrive. Later Dr. Aeschlimann joined us and shared the bench with me. Other chemists who were installed there were Dr. Martha Creighton, Dr. Herbert Fox, Dr. Oppenheimer, who died very shortly afterwards in the Coconut Grove fire in Boston, Dr. Leo Flexser, and Dr. John Plati, later also Dr. William E. (Bill) Scott, who arrived in August, and Dr. Lester Mischa Jampolsky (generally called Jamp), who arrived in September.

The plans for the Chemical Research Department made provision for a junior chemist (master or bachelor) and a lab assistant for every Ph.D. research chemist. In the beginning, all the research chemists (Ph.D.) transferred from Switzerland reported directly to Dr. Hans Heinz Wüest. As my first assignment, I was asked to compare various samples of commercial beta-ionone in order to establish which could be best used as starting material for the synthesis of vitamin A. This was not a very difficult task since physicochemical methods (UV spectra) gave clear answers about the positions of the double bonds in the long aliphatic side chain and about the purity of the product. The next project concerned the synthesis of water-soluble arsenicals which might be usable in the treatment of syphilis and would compete with Mapharsan, which just has been introduced. Our third project was the synthesis of coumarin-like compounds which were used as anticoagulants ("blood thinners"), like Heparin. All three projects did not give very exciting results and were abandoned after a relatively short time.

In his first months in the Nutley laboratory, Sternbach had neither a real professional challenge nor any noteworthy success. This rather negative period in his research was mirrored in his relationships at work. Sternbach did not get on at all with Wüest, his immediate superior; indeed, as he himself admits, he began to hate him. Sternbach questioned his boss's qualifications as a chemist. His complaints bore fruit and he was assigned to a new manager in December 1941, Dr. W.W. Goldberg, newly arrived from Basel. Salomon Kaiser was his junior chemist and Naomi Gottfried his laboratory assistant.

This was no improvement. Sternbach had been a colleague of Goldberg's in Zurich and held him in high esteem, but here found him opinionated and a hindrance to his work. The Director of Research, Dr. John Aeschlimann, whom Sternbach respected, released Sternbach from this collaboration with Goldberg. In general, Sternbach was very critical of superiors, especially those trained as chemists, and extremely demanding toward his subordinates. Critical, demanding, and implacable, occasionally unfair as well, Sternbach puts it in a nutshell: "Those who were above me were not my favorites."

He never doubted his ability in chemical matters. He demanded respect from his bosses in the form of support and from his subordinates in the form of loyal assistance. He wanted to be independent so that he could choose and consistently pursue what he regarded as the right path. He concealed his drive for unconditional freedom behind a warm amiability, and his proud self-confidence behind a charming modesty. This is not a contradiction. Sternbach was and is convinced of his qualities as a scientist and researcher. He is kindness and modesty personified. These traits exist alongside one another; their sum is a confident person at ease with himself. When his anger was aroused and he exploded, usually accompanied by a string of expletives, often in Polish and forceful, it was a genuine emotional outburst and did not last long. Kindness and the desire for harmony quickly regained the upper hand. He avoided open clashes whenever possible. What counted for him was the professional interest, which in his case was and is always a matter of conviction. This was also the driving force behind his pioneering achievements.

Sternbach worked for a while with Goldberg to develop the syntheses for vitamin A. But they abandoned this project after Dr. Otto Isler at Roche in Basel developed an effective method. Sternbach and Isler had a very friendly relationship.

Changes in Private Life

In 1943 the Sternbachs moved from their rented accommodations to their own home in Upper Montclair—a Tudor-style house at 10 Woodmont Road, which they bought for $10,000 and where they still live in great comfort and ease. With a garden, of course, and a garage which has been Herta Sternbach's exclusive domain since Leo reached his later years and began to lose his wife's confidence at the wheel. After several minor mishaps, Herta Sternbach overruled her husband's protests and revoked Leo's driving privileges, taking exclusive control of the car. From that point on, she began driving Leo to the laboratory and back every day, in part as an exercise in damage control, and in part as an act of love.

Their elder son was born on October 15, 1943, and christened Michael after his paternal grandfather. Their second son, Daniel, was born on May 28, 1949. When World War II ended in 1945, Sternbach's mother was able to emerge from her hiding place with Catholic friends in Krakow and, thanks to the intercession of Roche, move to Switzerland, where she lived with Herta Sternbach's mother in Zurich until 1948, when she joined her son and daughter-in-law in Upper Montclair. Herta's mother also came over for a year to help her daughter with the household after Daniel's birth.

Herta was largely responsible for the children's upbringing. Their father did not evade his parental duties; he found time to play with Michael and Daniel and devoted himself to them during the family vacations. But that did not alter the fact that Herta essentially took care of the family, the household, and everyday problems, leaving her husband free to focus on his research and later to undertake his many travel commitments. The children were brought up as Protestants but raised without emphasis on religion.

Herta Sternbach became a U.S. citizen in 1946 and Leo a year later.

The Laboratory as a Place of Fulfillment

In Nutley, Sternbach, who had been a research chemist since Basel, was promoted to Group Chief, a position that he held until 1959. In those 19 years he discovered a new synthesis of biotin, the ganglionic blocker

Arfonad (for limiting bleeding during brain surgery), and the tranquilizers Librium and Valium, achievements of extraordinary signifi-
cance. In terms of scientific effort and economic effect, this was far more
than might be expected of a chemist in the course of an average working career. And these were just the first fruits of a tremendous harvest.

Sternbach's ambition was focused on his laboratory work. He did not
have any career ambitions—quite the opposite. For he feared that every
rung he climbed up the ladder would remove him further from the
laboratory.

His account of the discovery of biotin records his dedicated approach
to research, which he pursued with perfectionism, objectivity, and
rationality. Biotin, a vitamin of the B complex, fulfills important biochemical functions in the metabolism of fat and carbohydrates and in
breaking down amino acids. Deficiency symptoms are not known to
occur spontaneously among adults. However, artificial nutrition can
result in a biotin deficiency. Indications include nonspecific symptoms,
such as tiredness, sleepiness, muscle pain, loss of appetite, and, above
all, dermatitis. Infants with a congenital defect in their metabolism
exhibit these skin changes, accompanied by loss of hair. These children
lack an enzyme (biotinides) that releases protein-bound biotin for use
by the body. Giving these children free biotin ensures their survival.
Biotin also plays an important role in animal breeding.

Nowhere is Sternbach more precise, detailed, and involved than in
his descriptions of chemical processes, as in the following example from
his notes on the synthesis of biotin:

> *We started our synthetic work in February 1943 and realized after the
> very first steps that we would face great difficulties, since the reaction
> products were extremely water-soluble, which made their isolation very
> difficult.*
>
> *Since the synthesis of mesodiaminosuccinic acid (2, R = H) was
> also quite involved, we decided to prepare this product in a novel way.
> We planned to start with dibromosuccinic acid, which could be read-*

ily prepared by the addition of bromine to fumaric acid, and to convert this product by treatment with benzylamine into dibenzylaminosuccinic acid. This acid we planned to debenzylate in the usual manner by hydrogenolysis using a palladium catalyst.

The preparation of dibenzylaminosuccinic acid worked very well and we obtained the product in rather good yield. However the next step, the formation of the imidazoline ring, caused considerable difficulties. We found that phosgene (in toluene solution) had to be used (diethylcarbonate did not react) and that the amount of this reactant had to be practically titrated in order to obtain acceptable yields, and these were only around 30%. Neither an excess of phosgene nor larger amounts of the cheap benzylamino-derivative increased the yield noticeably. Quite the contrary, the only result was the formation of ever increasing amounts of amorphous impurities, which were almost impossible to remove. We had to settle for the above mentioned yield of about 30%.

We continued our synthesis with this product, and left the removal of the benzyl groups to a later point. We converted quantitative yields of 3 into the anhydride 4, which crystallized well, by boiling its solution in acetic anhydride. We attempted its reduction to the lactone treatment with amalgamated zinc filings in a boiling mixture of acetic acid and acetic anhydride. Although we did obtain a product that crystallized beautifully, it was not the expected lactone. The structure determination showed that it was a completely unexpected product: it was the acetyl ester of the cyclized aldehydo acid.

In order to obtain sufficient amounts of starting materials we arranged the scale-up in the Pilot Plant and assisted Mr. Jensen, a Dane, a very competent plant chemist, who was in charge of the production. Coworker was Vincent Guroski, who did much of the work with me.

We prepared quite large amounts of 3 in an enameled open kettle. For the next step, the ring closure with phosgene (dissolved in toluene), we used a large walk-in hood and stirred the reaction mixture by hand *with a wooden paddle, being careful not to inhale too much of the phosgene.*

We found that the preparation of 5, which needed 2-3 hours in a vigorously stirred three-neck flask, took much longer when larger quantities were prepared in a large kettle with much slower stirring. We also had to use zinc dust instead of zinc chips in order to achieve the desired reduction.

Since it was known that aldehydes could be transformed into thioaldehydes through treatment with hydrogen sulfide and hydrogen chloride gas, we decided to convert our cyclic aldehydo derivative into the free aldehydo acid, transform this into the thioaldehyde or its polymer and, without isolating it, to reduce it with sodium sulfide to the thiol which we expected would cyclize to the thiolactone 6.

These reactions worked miraculously well (probably via a polythioaldehyde, a disulfide, and the free thiol acid) and yielded the desired thiolactone (6) in good yield. This product could be readily reacted with 3-ethoxypropyl-magnesium bromide to yield the product 7, which could be dehydrated and hydrogenated to yield the ethoxypropyl derivative (9). Instead of the expected bromopropyl derivative, the treatment of this product with hydrogen bromide in acetic acid produced a water-soluble product, which was discovered to be a thiophanium derivative that crystallized well (10). We decided to use this compound for the resolution. We reacted it with silver d-camphorsulfonate (prepared from silver hydroxide and d-camphorsulfonic acid) and separated the stereoisomeric camphorsulfonates by crystallization. The levorotary isomer (11) was then converted into a malonic ester (12), which, on being heated with hydrobromic acid, was simultaneously hydrolized, decarboxylated, and debenzylated to yield biotin (13) in an overall yield (starting with 1) of 4.1%, which is unbelievably superior to the published Merck and Lederle yields of 0.43 and 0.6% respectively. It was patented in 1949.

The accessibility of biotin induced us to include this vitamin in our multivitamin preparations, which was a real windfall since it forced all the other producers of multivitamin preparations to also include biotin, which they had to buy from us. This accessibility also enabled us to prepare biotin oxidation and reduction products and higher or lower homologs of biotin. They were all submitted for biological testing for biotin and antibiotin activity but did not show anything of practical value.

R = CH$_2$C$_6$H$_5$
Ac = CH$_3$CO
X = d – Camphorsulfonate ion

Breakthrough

The discovery of biotin propelled Sternbach into the select group of top researchers at Roche. The discovery of Arfonad, a ganglionic blocker used to limit bleeding during brain surgery, reinforced his reputation. Librium followed 4 years later, which introduced him to the wider world, where his fame was heightened by Quarzan (1960), Librax (1961) and, irrevocably, the blockbuster Valium Roche in 1963. This was not the end. He continued to produce successful research without interruption for more than 20 years, discovering drugs such as Mogadon (1965), Nobrium (1968), Dalmane (1970), Lexotanil (1974), Klonopin (1975), Rohypnol (1975), and Versed (1985).

This leads to the question of the prerequisites and talents that enabled this particular chemist to inaugurate a new era in research and therapy.

The Inventor's Discovery of Librium

Sternbach trusted in empirical methods. Although he referred to them as "old-fashioned," he knew from experience that there could be no doubt about their efficacy. He combined his conviction about empirical science and traditional methods with an inventor's vision. With both feet planted firmly on the ground, in his research he focused on revolutionary developments.

The starting point for Sternbach's work on benzodiazepines was tranquilizers, which at the time were still a new group of therapeutic preparations. In view of their clinical importance, Roche decided to focus on intensive, innovative research in this field. With the results of the pharmacologic tests on sedatives and tranquilizers in hand, the chemists at Roche were given the task of finding a new preparation that possessed the required properties, could be patented, and represented a qualitative improvement on tranquilizers. Sternbach has recorded these experiences with scientific accuracy and precision in the "Benzodiazepine

Story," which the company's in-house publishing arm, Editiones Roche, published in English and German.

Success depended on a preliminary decision about the choice of starting materials. Sternbach carefully considered the possibilities, weighing the advantages and disadvantages of molecular modification, synthesis of compounds, and a creative search for a new type of tranquilizer.

Although molecular modification as such is reliable, Sternbach decided against it. He wanted to use methods that were more innovative and more chemically interesting. Heightening his challenge was the fact that, at that time almost nothing was known about the chemical processes of the brain. This left Sternbach with the attractive, but demanding, creative path of accepting the challenge of finding a new type of tranquilizer and working with a new class of agents with unknown biological characteristics.

This decision encapsulates Sternbach's singularity. On the one hand, he took up a huge challenge with passion, confidence, and farsightedness and, on the other, he chose to go it alone in an entirely new area of research. Analogously, Sternbach took a similar bold and sure-footed approach in his private life. Sternbach is an excellent bridge player, but also a passionate mountain climber, who slowly but steadily rises higher and higher, whether on foot or on skis, overcoming risks with conviction, confidence and self-assurance to reach the summit safely.

Sternbach was looking for compounds that fulfilled various criteria: they had to be relatively unresearched, easily accessible, raise really challenging problems for the chemist, and offer a potentially diverse range of variants and transformations. Finally, the compounds had to allow for the possibility of biological activity.

To reach the future, Sternbach took a detour via the past. He recalled a few substances that he had discovered 20 years earlier while working as an assistant at the University of Krakow.

He writes in the "Benzodiazepine Story":

At the time we were looking for new azo dyes or interesting dye stuff intermediates, and came across some substances known as 4,5-benzo-

[hept-1,2,6-oxdiazines] in the German literature. From a chemical point of view, they were very interesting. They were formed in good yields and by interesting chemical reactions, but unfortunately did not lend themselves to transformation into usable dyes. With regret we dropped this group of compounds and turned to other things.

What Sternbach had sown in vain in Krakow gradually ripened in Nutley and produced a rich harvest. This was also possible because the papers Sternbach and his supervisor Prof. Karol Dziewoński published in Polish drew no reaction in the scientific literature. "However," as Sternbach noted in the "Benzodiazepine Story," "in 1954, shortly after we had started our investigations, Ried and Stahlhofen published a paper in which they described the synthesis of some other representatives of this series and some transformations, which in their view confirmed the heptoxdiazine structure of these compounds."

The compounds fulfilled all of the criteria that Sternbach had formulated when he embarked on his benzodiazepine research. But there had been a mistake. In a stringent criticism of his own work, Sternbach had to admit that he had been unable to achieve the results he had hoped for, let alone the pharmacological evidence to back them up. As though this disappointment were not enough, he lost the confidence of his superior, who felt Sternbach was barking up the wrong tree and demanded that he abandon his work. The change of priorities forced Sternbach to cut back his activities. Not only that, but urgently needed working space in the laboratory had to be freed up, which required a radical clearing out on his part. Sometimes luck enters through the back door and determines from that vantage point who is right and who is wrong.

In April 1957, in the course of obeying the order to tidy up, something wonderful happened. As Sternbach notes in the "Benzodiazepine Story":

During this procedure, Earl Reeder, my coworker, drew my attention to a few hundred milligrams of two products, a nicely crystallized base and its hydrochloride. The base was produced in 1955 . . . and its hydrochloride in 1956. Pharmacological tests had not been run on these products at the time, as we were busy with other problems. Because they were pure and had the expected composition, instead of throwing them away, we submitted the water-soluble salt for pharmacological testing. We thought that the expected negative pharmacological result would cap our work on this series of compounds, and perhaps provide enough for a chemical publication. We had no idea that this would be the start of a program that would keep us occupied for years to come.

Product trials began in May 1957. An enthusiastic pharmacologist, Dr. Lowell O. Randall, was able to announce that "in tests used for initial trials of tranquilizers and sedatives, the compound exhibited unusually interesting qualities." The breakthrough for Librium had taken place.

Research scientists include both loners and team workers. Sternbach belonged to both categories. He did not hesitate to follow the path that he thought right. With astuteness and energy, he overcame all resistance and obstacles, regardless of whether they had to do with chemistry, personnel, or hierarchy. He fought with heart and mind, but never with elbows or career-driven ambition. For this reason, he could also be a brilliant team worker. He fostered colleagues at all levels. He worked extremely closely with the pharmacologists, supported them, and was open in his communications with them. This openness also characterized his contacts with the lawyers in the patent department. He built bridges to them, motivated by curiosity and kindness.

Sternbach and his colleagues in the patent law department became a virtual factory, launching a tremendous number of patents and products over a period of 25 years.

Chapter 5

Upholding Success

Trusting to Chance

Sternbach's explanations for his success are low-key. He points to chance, though admits that this is not just a stroke of luck. He believes it is possible to create conditions that make it more likely for chance to occur and to influence one's lot in life.

Sternbach's influence on these preconditions was twofold. On the one hand, there was his hands-on, technical interest in the practice of chemistry, in the boiling, mixing, evaporating, and crystallizing. He also demanded proficiency at this level from his coworkers. On the other hand, and above all, there was his sheer joy in chemistry. People who bring pleasure, enthusiasm, and satisfaction to their job work more intensely. The result of such intensity is a greater number of combinations and compounds, which, in keeping with the law of greater numbers, leads to more substances worthy of pharmacological analysis. This, in turn, increases the chances of success.

Sternbach never got used to working in accordance with a systematic, detailed plan. He worked in a pretty un-American way, from one day to the next. A pragmatist, calm and collected, he took things as they came. At the same time, it would be wrong to assume that his guiding principle was hope, that he went to work without any inner commitment or professional ambition. He possessed an infallible feel for what was right. He rejected theory-based working hypotheses, trusting instead to fascination. Anything that grabbed him emotionally or fired his intuition aroused his interest, his drive, and his exceptional—and subsequently legendary—tenacity.

You could tell that he had his own way of working simply from looking at the chaos of his laboratory table. Colleagues never forgot it for the rest of their lives—even Karl Hürlimann, his first assistant at Roche, who complained about it to Herta Sternbach, and was given a sympathetic hearing. Sternbach's work area was an extravagance of test tubes and Erlenmeyer flasks left to their own resources to produce the desired crystals one day. Sternbach wrote up his research reports absolutely correctly, although they were thoroughly confusing for everybody else; sometimes he started at the front of the notebook, sometimes at the back. Order out of chaos! Here was an artist at work, a chemist who turned his laboratory into a studio where he produced masterpieces.

Career and Family as Existential Necessities

Sternbach is directly responsible for 240 patents, covering 5,093 patent rights abroad. When he retired in 1973, 4,380 were still in force, almost one fifth of all Roche patents at the time.

His discoveries did not earn him millions. For Librium and Valium he received the maximum annual bonuses of $10,000 on top of his normal salary. That was the rule, and Sternbach had no desire to be an exception. But he is pleased that his generous pension alleviated any financial worries. Material wealth has never been his goal in life.

He sought happiness in his work. And in his family. To recharge his batteries he went mountain climbing or skiing. Engadin, in the southern part of Switzerland, became his favorite place for relaxation. He has always enjoyed swimming in the sea. And he can go into raptures about good food. When visiting Roche's headquarters in Basel he never missed the "Sternbach Menu" at the Euler Hotel: veal with morels, dark brown rösti (fried grated potatoes), and Zuger tart, a confection with Kirschwasser, a fine Swiss liquor, for dessert.

Liberal and Tolerant

Michael K. Sternbach on His Father

Michael K. Sternbach and his wife Rosemary live in Little Silver, New Jersey. After studying chemistry, the older of Leo Sternbach's two sons took a degree in German Studies and European History. He worked as a sales representative for Roche for 30 years before retiring in 2002.

Michael Sternbach ascribes his father's success to happiness and love. He found happiness in his work and in his family. And he is in love with his wife, his two sons, and chemistry.

He not only loved the last, but had a grasp that went right to the roots of the subject. His father knew this, and he quickly taught people who was more knowledgeable when anybody tried to put obstacles in his path. However, he never took part in in-fighting, back-stabbing, or office politics, because he was simply not capable of it. When faced with opposition, his immediate reaction was one of indignation.

Leo Sternbach's character was molded by open thought and action, and by having to practice tolerance. His tolerant nature occasionally exhibited elements of fatalism, above all in his ability to accept reality without complaint. But once his sense of justice had been hurt, he re-sisted with outrage and courage, defending not only himself, but also his coworkers.

In the laboratory, the great chemist Leo Sternbach was extremely skillful in handling things. In daily life, however, he appears to be en-dowed with an extraordinary impracticality. His son Michael, for ex-ample, portrays his father as a naturally bad driver who was repeatedly involved in small and comical car accidents. In despera-tion, his mother had no other choice but to ban him from driving and ensure he never took the wheel.

The Right Thing at the Right Time

Daniel D. Sternbach on His Father

Daniel D. Sternbach, his wife Wiwi, and their daughters Laura und Emilie live in Chapel Hill, North Carolina. Like his father, whom he often visited in his laboratory as a child, he received a doctorate in chemistry. He studied at Rochester University, Brandeis University, and the Federal Institute of Technology (ETH) in Zurich. Since 1979, he has worked for GlaxoSmithKline in diabetes research.

Daniel appraises his father as an outstanding chemist. His strengths include an ability to comprehend chemistry from the inside out, to work with concentration, and to do the right thing at the right time. He has enormous self-confidence. And he has a great love of his profession. Although chemistry was the center of his father's life—his mother had to take care of the practical, daily concerns of life—the family and its harmony and well-being were extremely important for his father.

His strong, unshakeable self-confidence enabled Leo Sternbach to categorize his antagonists and opponents as ignoramuses, even idiots. This attitude made it easier for him to stick consistently to the path that he had recognized to be the right one.

In Daniel Sternbach's view, his father continued to go to his office at Roche in Nutley every day until well into his 94th year because being part of a world of work had its social attractions. Anyway, his father always felt happiest in a jacket and tie. Of course, it is also true that Leo Sternbach has always been blessed with a stupendous intellectual vitality. One sign of this is his love of bridge, which he has played all his life. Today he also plays this demanding game on his PC—which he needs someone to help him start.

Crowning Achievement and Irritation

The pharmacological fruits of Sternbach's genious—most notably Librium and Valium—were not only among the most successful prescription medicines of their time, but the benzodiazepine class as a whole proved to have tremendous and longstanding medical value. Knowing Sternbach and his deep motivation to reduce human suffering, one would wish that his invention was an unblemished gift to the world. But as life so often goes, things were not so black or white.

While Sternbach's discovery of Librium and Valium received enormous praise through the years from medical professionals and patients whose lives were enhanced by them, his invention was also immortalized in ways that were not always so favorable, bringing much attention to the problems of overprescribing and dependence. In 1966 Jacqueline Susann's treatment of self-medication in her novel *Valley of the Dolls* focused on this controversy. The theme continued in 1967 when the Rolling Stones released their album *Flowers*, one track of which, "Mother's Little Helper," chronicled the rampant consumption of Valium by harried housewives. U.S. politicians soon raised allegations that Librium and Valium led to dependence and called for drastic measures to curtail them.

"He Was Like a Father to Me"

Carl Mason, Laboratory Assistant, about His Boss

Carl Mason lives in retirement in Montclair, New Jersey. After completing military service, he went back to high school and subsequently studied mathematics and chemistry, but did not complete his degree. He got a job with Roche as a laboratory assistant and was part of the inner circle of Leo Sternbach's research team.

Carl Mason portrays his boss as full of ideas and absolutely sure about his methods. His command of crystallization was unequalled. He worked with precision and concentration. Accordingly, he knew he could be sure of management's recognition, especially after the discovery of Librium and Valium, when he basked in general esteem. This is exactly what counted for Leo Sternbach: the appreciation, the admiration, and the publicity all meant far more to him than any financial gain.

Carl Mason, for whom Valium is also a part of his own life's work, praises Leo Sternbach's decency, which he maintained even in an environment of envy and animosity. He never saw his boss frustrated or enraged and never saw him hurt others. On the contrary, fairness was the rule in his team. Leo Sternbach also took an interest in the personal problems of his co-workers, even to the extent of giving them financial support if necessary. Mason emphasizes: "He was like a father to me and did what he could."

In recollecting Leo Sternbach, Mason also recalls a good organizer who wanted competent people around him, a man able to successfully motivate and structure his group, and a perfectionist who also had his moments as an absent-minded professor.

Asked why Leo Sternbach still visited his office decades after his retirement, Mason alludes to the economic triumph of Sternbach's discoveries: "He goes in to the house he built."

Golden Age

The Pharmacologist Barel Kappell
on the Chemist Leo Sternbach

Barel Kappell and her husband live in Essex Fells, New Jersey. She studied pharmacology at Decatur College, Georgia, and worked at Roche from 1949–1981.

Kappell calls the period of research leading up to Librium and Valium the "golden age." The collaboration between her, her boss Lowell Randall, and Leo Sternbach functioned perfectly. In this triangle, it was important for Leo Sternbach that everybody exchanged information willingly and in detail. Lowell Randall, in turn, gave absolute priority to Librium and Valium. This cooperative atmosphere created the excellent conditions for Kappell's pharmacological studies that helped to bring the research to a successful conclusion.

Humanitarian Duty

It's a fact that Sternbach's invention generated intense social and political attitudes about psychiatric drugs. Sternbach himself, as well as Roche, recognized that these were prescription drugs whose use needed to be authorized by a responsible physician, and that uncontrolled use should be avoided. Sternbach always took exception, and strongly objects to this day, to the notion that inventions like his, which are intended to treat people in need and are immensely effective when appropriately used, should be restricted or eliminated because of reckless misuse. The suggestion of such an approach immediately raises the characteristic Sternbach ire, which rears its head whenever his view of obvious common sense is breached. As a morally rooted chemist and scientist, his work in the service of the sick was a humanitarian duty. Whenever the discussion turns to criticism of psychiatric drugs, which do so much good and offer such tremendous relief to so many in need, Sternbach cannot comprehend the venom of the attacks against these medicines. For him, the conclusion is simple: It would be wrong to deprive the many of available benefits because of the inappropriate and ill-advised actions of the few.

Proud of Public Recognition

The Chemist Earl Reeder on the Chemist Leo Sternbach

Earl Reeder and his wife live in Nutley, New Jersey, where the Roche Pharmaceuticals Division has its U.S. headquarters. He graduated from college as a pharmaceutical technician, studied chemistry during his military service, and later earned a Bachelor of Science degree. In 1952 he joined Roche and until his retirement worked exclusively with Leo Sternbach, initially as a laboratory assistant and then as a chemist. The friendship that developed out of this relationship continues to this day.

Yes, Earl Reeder says, he was actually the co-discoverer of Librium and Valium. But given his lack of ambition, he never placed any value on this. Public recognition was essential for Leo Sternbach, but not for him. This modesty probably has something to do with the fact that success in benzodiazepine research was not always the result of purposeful efforts, but instead often of chance. Incidentally, he would like to mention that he has 30 scientific publications and 30 co-registered patents to his name. And that is enough for him.

To nip all doubts in the bud, he does not hesitate to state that there is more to Leo Sternbach than just ambition. He is an outstanding chemist, a fine man, and a fair and courageous boss who impressively refused to become involved in intrigues.

He had only one striking weakness: driving. On skis he was as wild as he was at the steering wheel, but with considerably fewer accidents.

The Reeders and the Sternbachs are members of the same bridge club, where they still get together.

Sternbach himself has withdrawn from scientific discourse. Since his time the field has changed completely. His kind of chemistry has had its day; today's chemistry is different. People like Sternbach who have made progress possible have the satisfaction of knowing that progress is now the responsibility of younger generations. He assumes that his successors and their successors are making the right decisions. There is no lamenting the bygone days or regret that times have changed. What inspired him continues. Age has not taken him prisoner. In age he is as he has always been: an exceptionally free spirit.

Direct and Honest

The Laboratory Technician Barbara C. Sluboski
on her Boss, Leo Sternbach

Barbara C. Sluboski and her husband live in Matawan, New Jersey. She worked for Leo Sternbach at Roche in Nutley from 1960 to 1962 and again from 1970 until her retirement in 1998.

Barbara Sluboski puts great emphasis on Herta Sternbach's signifi-cance and influence. She not only took care of the family and house-hold, but her husband always asked her advice: "I have to check with Herta." Sluboski found that the two of them were ideal parents: sym-pathetic, generous, and ready to help financially.

In the close working group that consisted of Earl Reeder, Carl Mason, and Sluboski, Leo Sternbach was highly respected. He was enthusias-tic, open, never bad tempered or impatient, and always full of ques-tions. He dealt with problems efficiently, often bypassing the official channels. He was obstinate, fired by optimism, self-confident, trusted his instincts, and was an unshakeable realist: "Life is how it is."

Leo Sternbach said what he thought; with his directness and honesty he was not what is known today as "politically correct."

He regarded his closest co-workers as friends, and regularly invited them to the house and to the Sternbach's summer vacation home.

Leo Sternbach was always simple and modest. He wore the same jacket for years, and only occasionally changed his tie. What was impor-tant for him was the reality, not the appearance.

Part II

The Drug That Changed the World

Chapter 6

The Benzodiazepine Story

E very day millions of people around the world take a benzodiazepine medication prescribed for them by their doctor. These medications bring vast improvements in the quality of life for those suffering from debilitating anxiety and related disorders; without these medicines their family, social, and working lives would be seriously curtailed.

Drugs in the benzodiazepine family also bring rapid and effective relief from severe sleep disorders, which also can have devastating effects on people's lives.

Benzodiazepines, as tablets, injections or continuous infusions, are vital, too, as anticonvulsants, notably for the treatment of status epilepticus (life-threatening prolonged or recurrent seizures); they are used as sedatives in many obstetric and gynecologic procedures (and as treatment for potentially deadly eclamptic seizures during pregnancy); they may be used as premedication before surgical operations and in anesthesia; and they can provide long-term calming for seriously ill patients being treated in intensive care units.

They also find uses as muscle relaxants in sports medicine, in the treatment of childhood epilepsy, and in the management of alcohol and heroin addiction (although all these uses may not necessarily be licensed or approved in all countries).

All in all, the benzodiazepines have come a long way since Leo Sternbach synthesized the first of them, chlordiazepoxide, in his laboratory in 1955. For nearly 50 years since then, they continue to be among the most widely prescribed drugs in the world. Nothing has yet replaced them for the safe and effective treatment of anxiety and related disorders. One of them, diazepam, continues to be featured on the World Health Organization's Model List of "essential" medicines.

In addition to their effectiveness, perhaps the main reason the benzodiazepines were welcomed so positively when they were first introduced was their safety. As we shall see later in this section of the book, they were infinitely safer than the drugs that had preceded them. Their use in general medicine, as well as in psychiatry, increased enormously in the 20 years following the introduction of chlordiazepoxide as Librium in 1960, so that by the late 1970s drugs such as diazepam (Valium Roche) were the most highly prescribed drugs in the world for the treatment of conditions affecting the central nervous system. As Dr. Adam Doble commented in a book on the benzodiazepines[1] in 1998: "Their perceived effectiveness as anxiolytics and sleeping pills and their lack of life-threatening side-effects or toxicity on overdose was perhaps unique amongst all psychotropic drugs."

Another perception, however, was also gaining ground. Many general practitioners, and certainly many members of the public, were coming to regard the benzodiazepines as a universal panacea for the stresses and strains of everyday life. This perception led in many cases to the prescription of benzodiazepines not for specific, well-defined conditions, nor for short periods of time, but to long-term and somewhat indiscriminate prescribing. In the immortal words of the Rolling Stones' song, benzodiazepines (particularly Valium) had become "mother's little helpers."

We might remember, too, films such as *Fame* (1980) and the song line "I'm gonna live forever." There was a feeling, among younger people particularly, that they were immortal and that they should strive for physical and psychological perfection. If you were not part of this psychologically perfect elite then you might consider yourself a failure, a reject.

So there was considerable pressure on people to maintain membership of this group. In some quarters at least, benzodiazepines were often seen as drugs that enabled people to fit more comfortably in this stress-free, perfection-seeking social milieu.

This raised concerns by some physicians, notably Professor Malcolm Lader in the United Kingdom, that benzodiazepines were becoming "the opium of the masses" and that many people who took them did not need them for a recognizable, defined medical condition.

In the early 1980s, other scientists and researchers were beginning to raise concerns that the benzodiazepines could cause problems of dependence. They put forward evidence of withdrawal symptoms, seen in certain patients when the medication was stopped, particularly after longer-term use. There was also evidence that benzodiazepines could become drugs of abuse, although this problem was largely confined to those who were already abusing other drugs.

By the mid-1980s such concerns, and the publicizing of them (both to the medical profession and to the public) led to increasing restrictions on the use of benzodiazepines, notably in the United Kingdom, but also in the United States and elsewhere in the world. This in turn prompted an increasing reluctance among doctors to prescribe them.

Cultural factors also influenced a more negative approach to the use of the benzodiazepines and heightened opposition to them. There had always been a tendency in some countries to view anxiety syndromes as less than serious diseases, as minor neuroses from which the patient could recover through some effort of will. In other words, anxiety disorders were not regarded as illnesses, but simply signs of weakness of character. Although this is both untrue and offensive (anxiety disorders are not trivial and they should not be trivialized), such attitudes undeniably played their part in promoting stronger restrictions on benzodiazepine use.

The consequence of official regulations, restrictive guidelines and negative pressure from the public and members of the medical profession led to a situation in which physicians were often reluctant to prescribe benzodiazepines, even for patients who clearly needed them, and in which patients were reluctant to take them, through an unfounded fear of "addiction." Not surprisingly, this led to a major decline in benzodiazepine prescribing in the 1990s.

This, in turn, led to severe undertreatment of anxiety and related disorders around the world, to the detriment of public health. Furthermore, when patients *do* receive medication, it is often with drugs that do not have proven efficacy, which are less well tolerated by patients, and which have more adverse effects than the benzodiazepines.

The pressure on benzodiazepines led to intensive investigations of alternatives (such as venlaflaxine, buspirone, and the selective serotonin reuptake inhibitor [SSRI], group of drugs) in some anxiety disorders. None of them, however, have the speedy onset of action of the benzodiazepines, and these drugs have high numbers of nonresponders.

So, from an apparently overly enthusiastic use of the benzodiazepines, it now seems that the pendulum of opinion has swung too far in the opposite direction. There is a need for reassessment, to put the advantages and disadvantages of the benzodiazepines into a proper perspective.

It is appropriate that part of this reassessment should take place in this section of the book, assessing the medical, scientific, and social impact of Leo Sternbach's great achievement in bringing to the world these drugs that have relieved the suffering of so many people.

The Need for the Benzodiazepines:
Before the Psychopharmacological Revolution

In looking at the impact of the benzodiazepines, it is worthwhile considering briefly the history of drug treatment for mental conditions in the past one hundred years or so.

At the beginning of the past century, there were *no* effective treatments for the major mental illnesses of dementia praecox (schizophrenia), manic–depressive insanity (bipolar mood disorder) or dementia paralytica (neurosyphilis). Confinement in an institution was the norm, and drugs such as the opiates, bromides, barbiturates, antihistamines, and chloral hydrate were used to reduce agitation and behavioral problems.

For the less serious "neuroses," among which are anxiety and related disorders, the accent was on "sedation" rather than on any attempt to get at underlying causes.

A few new therapies were introduced for psychotic illness in the early decades of the past century, such as deliberate infection with malaria to arrest the progress of neurosyphilis, and deep-sleep therapy for schizophrenia. Other radical therapies included insulin-induced coma, convulsive therapy, and leukotomy. Between the two world wars there was also an explosion of interest in psychoanalysis, following the insights of Sigmund Freud.

But it was not until the 1950s that the real revolution in the use of drugs to treat mental illness (psychopharmacology) began. It offered a more credible alternative to psychoanalysis, particularly for major psychoses.

This revolution started with new drugs to treat epilepsy, following the development, in the late 1930s, of techniques for assessing the anticonvulsant effects of chemical compounds more accurately. These showed the superior effects of phenytoin in one type of epilepsy (temporal lobe epilepsy) and prompted research that led to the discovery of other antiepileptic drugs, such as tridione and mysoline.

These successes spurred further efforts, spearheaded by pharmaceutical companies, to find compounds that affected the functioning of the brain and mental processes. Among the discoveries was a compound called chlorpromazine, which was synthesized in 1950 in the laboratories of the French pharmaceutical company Rhone-Poulenc (now part of Aventis). This drug was first used in surgery, to induce "artificial hibernation," but was later shown, in combination with electroconvulsive therapy (ECT) and pethidine, to reduce agitation in manic–

depressive patients. In 1952, two French doctors, Jean Delay and Pierre Deniker, systematically evaluated chlorpromazine as a single-drug therapy and showed that it had general antipsychotic effects—not only did it subdue agitation, but it also had positive effects on hallucinations, delirium, autism, and affective symptoms (i.e. those concerned with emotions rather than rational, intellectual thought).

Here at last was a drug with clear and direct effects on the brain and on mood disorders. This was the beginning of true psychopharmacology and the concept that a chemical compound could provide truly effective treatment for a psychiatric illness.

In 1952 it was also shown (by Max Lurie and Harry Salzer in Cincinnati) that a drug called isoniazid could be used as an antidepressant. In 1954 Nathan Kline in New York showed that extracts from the plant *Rauwolfia serpentina* had a therapeutic effect on both anxiety and obsessive–compulsive disorders, while Delay and Deniker (and others in the United States and Switzerland) reported that reserpine had a favorable effect on mania.

Earlier Treatments for Anxiety

Although the psychopharmacological revolution, as Deniker wrote in 1990, has "changed the face of madness" and transformed the "lunatic" into an ordinary patient, it was clear to both physicians and the public that the vast majority of "nervous" conditions in the community were not mood disorders, but rather various forms of anxiety. Until the 1950s the drugs that had been shown to be useful in these conditions were generally thought of as "sedatives."

As a World Health Organization expert report on anxiolytic drugs[2] points out: "Since ancient times man has searched for the means to allay his everyday worries, relieve feelings of inner anxiety and facilitate a restful sleep."

The earliest of these compounds, in Western civilizations at least, was alcohol (or more precisely ethyl alcohol) and it is still widely used today, whether beer, wine, or spirits, to ease tension and relieve anxiety. Physicians and medical researchers, however, recognize that in clinical terms the risks of alcohol consumption often far outweigh its advantages. The therapeutic value of alcohol is limited, it is difficult to get the dose right, it is dangerous in overdose, and long-term use produces a wide range of undesirable effects. Nonetheless, many physicians, along with many other people, still use alcohol as a way of relieving tension and anxiety.

In the latter half of the 19th century, bromide salts and compounds with effects similar to ethyl alcohol, such as paraldehyde and chloral hydrate, were introduced into medical practice as sedatives. As well as being extensively prescribed, they were also sold freely "over the counter" in many Western countries, promoting self-medication and long-term use.

Chloral hydrate was a drug much used (and abused) by artists and writers. The Victorian painter Dante Gabriel Rossetti is an interesting example: the effects of choral hydrate can be seen in his work. He started using the drug following the death of his wife and began, of course, by taking relatively low doses. At this point we see serene, religious paintings, such as St. Agnes at the spinning wheel, but as his chloral habit caught hold, and his daily dose rapidly escalated, more secular, voluptuous, almost hallucinatory, women begin to appear.

So, while drugs such a chloral hydrate worked (to a limited extent) as sedatives, they also led to psychological problems, as well as to the dangers of dependency and overuse. Unfortunately, it took many years for the seriousness of these adverse effects to be fully recognized. Similarly, it was not until the 1930s that it was fully acknowledged that the bromides had cumulative effects and that they could provoke toxic delirium. Paraldehyde also seemed to be able to induce psychotic states.

The clinical effectiveness of these older sedatives was limited, and as the medical profession and the public became aware of these serious unwanted effects, their use declined rapidly.

The dominant antianxiety (sedative) and sleeping (hypnotic) agents in the first half of the 20th century were the barbiturates, which were first introduced in 1900 (on St. Barbara's day, hence the name). Although these, too, had many serious side effects, they were used extensively and given to patients for long periods of time. It was not until the 1950s that there was widespread concern about their safety and their efficacy in dealing with anxiety.

It became clear that the antianxiety effects of the barbiturates were "nonspecific," that is, they were simply a part of a generalized depression of activity in the central nervous system. For most patients, it was not possible to relieve anxiety without producing unwanted sedation at the same time. In addition, barbiturates impaired people's intellectual and motor skills (the control over muscles and movement) so that when they were taking them, they were not functioning "normally," either mentally or physically.

There was also a considerable potential for abuse and addiction with the barbiturates, as well as the dangers of overdose. These drugs could kill at doses not much higher than those used in treatment, and deaths from barbiturate poisoning, both accidental and intentional, were far too common.

All these dangers and drawbacks led to a growing dissatisfaction with the use of barbiturates and intensified research efforts to find safer alternative drugs.

The first of these was meprobamate, synthesized in 1955 by Frank Berger at the Carter Wallace Laboratories in New Jersey and distributed by Carter Wallace and Wyeth.

Berger's work with meprobamate moved us forward from merely sedating anxious patients toward the concept of an anxiolytic, or "tranquilizer," which removed the symptoms of anxiety without undue sedation. Berger was explicitly trying to create a drug that would produce muscle relaxation and that, by inhibiting feedback from tense muscles, would reduce sufferers' perception of themselves as being "anxious."

Meprobamate rapidly became a best seller, with widespread use both in general practice and outpatient psychiatry. Experience over the next 10 years or so, however, showed that it was *not* dramatically less sedative than the barbiturates, that it was almost as dangerous in overdose, and that it was not much less addictive.

Medically and scientifically, the time was ripe for a tranquilizer that met Berger's criteria of antianxiety action without undue sedation. The benzodiazepines produced by Roche fulfilled that role: first with Librium (chlordiazepoxide), synthesized by Leo Sternbach in 1955 and introduced in 1960, then with Valium Roche (diazepam), launched in 1963, and subsequently with dozens of more effective drugs in the same family.

Although the term had been coined earlier to try to distinguish meprobamate from older sedatives, Librium and Valium Roche were the first true tranquilizers.

The terminology is somewhat confusing, because in the United States meprobamate and the benzodiazepines were soon classified as "minor tranquilizers," in contrast to mood-altering drugs, which were known as "major tranquilizers." In Europe and elsewhere, however, the mood-altering drugs are usually referred to as neuroleptics (a term proposed by Delay and Deniker in 1955, which means literally "taking hold of the nerves"), whereas benzodiazepines, in their antianxiety role, may simply be called tranquilizers or anxiolytics. And on the subject of names, benzodiazepines are relatively straightforward: their name derives from the fact that their core structure consists of a benzene ring fused to a diazepine ring.

The Advent of the Benzodiazepines

As with many major discoveries in science and medicine, there was an element of serendipity in the development of the first benzodiazepine, chlordiazepoxide, in 1955. It was created quite unintentionally: Leo Sternbach had set out to make something else, but the structure of the molecule changed unexpectedly during the process of synthesis.

Furthermore, Dr. Sternbach had not submitted these new compounds (he had created the water-soluble hydrochloride form of chlordiazepoxide in 1956) for pharmacological testing because he and his colleagues were concentrating on other problems. It was not until May 1957 that chlordiazepoxide hydrochloride was sent for tests, and even then Dr. Sternbach had few hopes that it would be an active compound with therapeutic potential; he thought he might just have enough data to publish some results in a chemistry journal!

But from the outset his fellow researchers and clinical colleagues at Roche were full of enthusiasm. Preliminary screening showed that chlordiazepoxide was much more effective than meprobamate (then enjoying considerable success as a tranquilizer) and toxicological tests showed that it was remarkably safe. Animal experiments demonstrated a profound calming effect. In one famous study, chlordiazepoxide was tested on leopards, lions, and tigers at the San Diego Zoo and the big cats were successfully subdued. One newspaper headline asked: "The Drug That Tames Tigers—What Will It Do for Nervous Women?" It should be pointed out, however, that Roche never officially marketed the drug in this way.

The animal studies were followed by clinical trials in humans, which showed how effective the new compound was in treating anxiety disorders and which confirmed its safety. The first clinical trials, in patients with schizophrenia, showed that while chlordiazepoxide had no true antipsychotic activity, it brought significant reductions in anxiety in these patients. In a further study, in what today would officially be termed "generalized anxiety disorder," it showed remarkable efficacy.

The researchers concluded that chlordiazepoxide "makes possible successful treatment of patients (with anxiety and tension states) who heretofore have been refractory to all other modalities of treatment." In other words, patients who had previously suffered without relief could now be treated successfully.

In 1960, less than two-and-a-half years after the first pharmacological tests, the new compound was brought to the market, as Librium. It was warmly welcomed by physicians—and their patients—and had a major impact on the treatment of anxiety disorders.

Such was its success that there was intense research activity to synthesize other compounds in the same family, with Leo Sternbach and his team at Roche at the forefront of this effort. Many other pharmaceutical companies also joined the hunt to create compounds with a similar therapeutic profile, and within the next three decades approximately 50 new benzodiazepine compounds were created. (Not all of these are still in use, but at the end of the 20th century 24 of them were still available in clinical practice in the United States, the United Kingdom, and France.)

In addition to their tranquilizing or antianxiety effects, benzodiazepines also have hypnotic (sleep-inducing), anticonvulsant, muscle-relaxing, and amnestic properties. Every benzodiazepine has these effects, but different chemical compounds in the benzodiazepine family promote each of these effects to a greater or lesser extent. Thus, one benzodiazepine may be more hypnotic, another more anxiolytic, and a third more anticonvulsant.

After Librium, Leo Sternbach and Roche were responsible for the creation of another 8 therapeutically active benzodiazepines, among them diazepam (Valium Roche). Diazepam turned out to be considerably more potent than chlordiazepoxide, in that there was a greater dissociation between its anxiolytic and sedative properties. It was marketed in the United States in 1963, and by the end of the 1960s it had become the best selling psychotropic ("mind-affecting") drug in the Western world.

One of us (K.R.) conducted one of the earliest trials of chlordiazepoxide (Librium) in the United States, and the results in overcoming crippling anxiety disorders were truly remarkable. The advent of Valium in the early 1960s finally allowed family doctors to treat anxious patients with a safe and effective medication, largely replacing psychotherapy or psychoanalysis, therapies that were rather ineffective and could be provided only by a psychiatric expert. Most important, family physicians for the first time had an effective and safe tool available to treat the many patients suffering from anxiety.

Dr. Rickels says:

I still remember some of my patients. Almost over night they lost their long-term and life-limiting disabilities. I never had one of my patients become dependent and develop withdrawal reactions, because I always tapered off the dose when stopping treatment. (This was long before we learned that some patients could become dependent on benzodiazepines.) My goal in therapy always was, and still is, to obtain the best results with the least amount and time on drug therapy. My goal was, and still is, to teach patients to cope better with life's many stresses, first under the protection of medication and later without medication, or perhaps only occasional use when needed.

In the 20 years or so following the introduction of Librium, many other important benzodiazepines, with different pharmacological properties, and thus different clinical indications (sleep induction, premedication, anticonvulsive, sedative and so on), were created by Leo Sternbach and his team at Roche. Here is a list of Benzodiazepines developed by Roche and their year of introduction

Librium	1960
Valium Roche	1963
Mogadon	1965
Nobrium	1968
Rivotril	1973
Lexotan	1974
Rohypnol	1975
Dalmadorm	1978
Dormicum	1982

In addition to their superior effectiveness in overcoming anxiety, it was their safety that made the benzodiazepines so useful when they were first introduced. There was a vast gain in therapeutic index (the balance between the efficacy and benefits of a drug and its adverse effects) compared with the previously available medications, including meprobamate and the barbiturates.

As we have seen, these earlier sedatives were dangerous in overdose, with a deadly progression from sedation to unconsciousness and then death from respiratory collapse. The barbiturates were particularly dangerous, and numerous deaths from overdose (both accidental and intentional) were reported.

With the benzodiazepines, these difficulties simply did not occur. Although increasing the dose of a benzodiazepine would put people to sleep (instead of a simple tranquilizing effect), they would wake up again in a relatively short time and recover fully. Deaths from an overdose of "sleeping pills" disappeared very quickly once the benzodiazepines were in widespread use (see Figure 6.1).

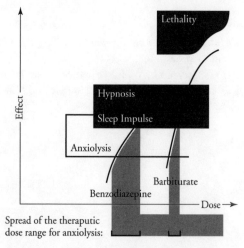

Figure 6.1 Spread of therapeutic dose range for benzodiazepines and the now obsolete barbiturates. (Source: *Moeller H-J, Rickels K.* Rational and Appropriate Prescribing of the Benzodiazepines, *The Media Alliance Partnership. Reprinted with permission.*)

This lack of life-threatening side effects or toxicity on overdose was unique among all psychotropic drugs available at that time. In fact, the benzodiazepines are possibly the least toxic drugs ever used in any branch of medicine, let alone psychiatry, and they have set a standard for safety by which all other psychotropic drugs have to be judged.

We now know that the safety of benzodiazepines is due to the way they act on a specific receptor in the nerve cells in the brain, but at the time of the introduction of the first benzodiazepines, and for some 15 years afterward, scientists and clinicians had no idea *why* benzodiazepines were so safe. They were just glad that they were.

So were the millions of patients around the world who were suffering from anxiety and related disorders. Before assessing the medical and social impact of the benzodiazepines, it is appropriate to look in some detail at these disorders and the problems they can cause in the lives of so many people.

References

1. Doble A. *The GABA/Benzodiazepine Receptor as a Target for Psychoactive Drugs.* Georgetown, TX: RG Landes, 1998.
2. Racagni C, Masotto C, Steardo L. WHO Expert Series on Neuroscience, Volume 3, *Pharmacology of Anxiolytic Drugs.* Geneva: Hogrefe and Huber, 1997.

Chapter 7

The Crippling Cost of Anxiety, and the Benzodiazepine Revolution

As we have already pointed out, anxiety disorders are not trivial. They are serious medical illnesses. They fill people's lives with overwhelming anxiety and fear. They are long-term, relentless, and if not treated, can grow progressively worse.

Anxiety disorders, which range from specific phobias to generalized anxiety disorder, are also very widespread. It is estimated by the National Institute of Mental Health (NIMH) in the United States, for example, that they affect approximately 19 million American adults. Yet only one in four of these people receives any kind of treatment for their condition.

According to the World Health Organization as many as 450 million people around the world are estimated to suffer from anxiety disorder at any given time.

The dry statistics, however, do not communicate what it *feels* like to be a sufferer from chronic anxiety. Here are some quotes, gathered by the NIMH, from sufferers from various types of anxiety disorder:

> "I always thought I was just a worrier. I'd feel keyed up and unable to relax. At times it would come and go, and at times it would be constant. It could go on for days." GENERALIZED ANXIETY DISORDER

"I have terrible sleeping problems. There were times when I would wake up wired in the middle of the night. I had trouble concentrating, even reading a newspaper or a novel. Sometimes I'd feel a little light-headed. My heart would race or pound—and that would make me worry more. I was always imagining things were worse than they really were: when I got a stomach ache, I would think it was an ulcer." GENERALIZED ANXIETY DISORDER

"For me, a panic attack is an almost violent experience, I feel disconnected from reality. I feel like I am losing control in a very extreme way. My heart pounds really hard, I feel like I can't get my breath and there is an overwhelming feeling that things are crashing in on me." PANIC DISORDER

"In between attacks there is this dread and anxiety that it is going to happen again. I am afraid to go back to the place where I have had an attack. Unless I get help, there soon won't be any place where I can go and feel safe from panic." PANIC DISORDER

"I couldn't do anything without rituals. They invaded every aspect of my life. I would wash my hair three times as opposed to once, because three was a good luck number and one wasn't. It took me longer to read because I would count the lines in a paragraph. When I set my alarm at night, I had to set it to a number that wouldn't add up to a 'bad' number." OBSESSIVE–COMPULSIVE DISORDER

"In any social situation, I felt fear. I would be anxious before I even left the house and it would escalate as I got closer to a college class, a party, or whatever. I would feel sick at my stomach—it almost felt like I had the flu. My heart would pound, my palms would go sweaty and I would get this feeling of being removed from myself and from everybody else." SOCIAL PHOBIA

"When I would walk into a room full of people, I'd turn red and it would feel like everybody's eyes were on me. I was embarrassed to stand off in a corner by myself, but I couldn't think of anything to say to anybody. It was humiliating. I felt so clumsy. I couldn't wait to get out." SOCIAL PHOBIA

Anxiety, or fear (we'll define these terms in a moment), is a normal emotional response to physical danger. It enables us, as Shakespeare put it, to "stiffen the sinews and summon up the blood" when danger threatens. This "fight or flight" response is still a useful defense mechanism, even though physical danger is uncommon for most of us. In evolutionary terms, of course, this response has been vital in ensuring that our species, and thousands of others, have survived through time.

In our modern lives we can see that this sort of response might also be useful in concentrating the mind when a task needs to be performed by a deadline, whether it is writing a report or being on time for a meeting. We might call the pressure we are under "stress." We recognize, too, that a degree of "nervousness" helps when we have to perform in front of other people, whether giving a presentation, going for a job interview, or even playing in a concert. It keys us up to give our best.

Anxiety disorders, however, are a far cry from these normal responses. They are *abnormal*, exaggerated, and prolonged responses, that linger on well after any threat has passed (if indeed a threat existed in the first place). In a word, they are inappropriate.

One of the difficulties in discussing the area of human emotions is that everyone has their own idea about what words like *stress, fear,* and *anxiety* mean. As scientists we need to try to be precise. We would like here to define *stress* as an external stimulus that signals danger, and often causes pain. *Fear* is the short-term response that such stress produces (both in humans and in laboratory animals). *Anxiety* exhibits many of the same symptoms as fear, but the feelings and the physical symptoms are exaggerated and they linger on long after the stress is gone and the threat has passed.

Let's take an everyday example. Suppose you receive a letter from your bank manager, saying that you are overdrawn and you are not going to have any more credit facilities. It might give you a bit of a shock. You would, quite rightly, worry about this, take it seriously, and try to do something about it, but the letter and its consequences would not occupy *all* your thoughts *all* the time.

For people suffering from anxiety, however, such a letter would invariably create a major and ongoing problem. Throughout the day they would turn their thoughts to the letter, mulling over all the details in their minds, worrying about what was going to happen (even envisaging being sent to court, being made bankrupt). At night too, and night after night, these anxious thoughts would keep them awake, tossing and turning. The sufferer from anxiety is overreacting, is not able to make a normal reaction to a commonplace, although admittedly unpleasant, event. And they would go on worrying for days, until the next stressful event came along to stimulate more agony.

As we have seen from the quotations above, such a long-term and exaggerated response leads to problems that cripple people's lives, preventing them from functioning properly as human beings. Their family relationships, their social lives, and their capacity to work are damaged, so that as well as a human and social cost, there is also a huge economic cost associated with anxiety disorders.

Defining Anxiety Disorders

As well as trying to define such concepts as fear and anxiety, the actual naming of mental diseases has also proved tricky, and through the years different names have been applied to the same conditions (or at least the same set of symptoms). Nomenclature and classification usually followed the preoccupations of particular countries or cultural groups, and their views of the underlying causes of illness.

Classification systems such as the International Classification of Diseases of the World Health Organization (ICD-10) or the Diagnostic and Statistical Manual of the American Psychiatric Association (DSM-IV) have been set up to try to overcome these differences and, by grouping together sets of signs and symptoms, to help physicians make diagnoses that have some international consistency.

As far as anxiety and related disorders are concerned, there is some general agreement about terms, although there may be differences of emphasis, particularly on opposite sides of the Atlantic. It should also be remembered that classification systems are seldom perfect and that patients coming to the doctor with real problems often do not present with signs and symptoms that make a diagnosis clear-cut. Indeed, patients often present with "mixed" syndromes (for instance, mixed anxiety and depression) that require skillful evaluation and careful selection of treatment.

As a framework for looking at the anxiety disorders we will use the ICD-10 and we'll concentrate on the following conditions:

- Generalized anxiety disorder
- Panic disorder
- Social phobia (and some other phobias)
- Obsessive–compulsive disorder
- Posttraumatic stress disorder
- Acute stress and adjustment disorders
- Somatoform disorders
- Sleep disorders

Generalized Anxiety Disorder

Generalized anxiety disorder (GAD) is a widespread condition and is frequently seen by primary care physicians ("family doctors," general practitioners). The NIMH estimates that 4 million adult Americans suffer from GAD, and there is no reason to suppose that prevalence rates are lower elsewhere in the world. Twice as many women as men consult a doctor about this problem and it comes on gradually. It can occur at anytime during a person's life, but it is most likely to develop between childhood and middle age.

In many psychological disturbances, the ratio of people seen by physicians seems to be about two-thirds women to one-third men. This is unlikely, however, to be a reflection of the true incidence of such conditions in the community, since the balance is tipped toward women because of a number of factors, many of them sociological. First, women are more used to being "medicalized." They see doctors in the normal course of pregnancy and they take their children to the doctors more often than their husbands (or male partners) do. Therefore, when they feel under stress, unable to cope, anxious, or depressed, they are more likely to go to the doctor than men are. Culturally, men are also more likely to have a "macho" reaction to anxiety and indeed to other psychological disturbances. They are much more likely, particularly in Anglo-Saxon cultures, to "grin and bear it" rather than to seek help. (They also tend to "self-medicate" with alcohol more than women do.) That said, there may in fact be genetic and hormonal factors that make women more prone than men to suffer from these disorders.

When (and if) people with GAD first come to the doctor, they are likely to report physical symptoms, such as headache or a pounding heart, or to say that they can't sleep properly. Deeper questioning by the doctor will reveal the psychic (mental) and somatic (physical) symptoms that are part of the whole picture of anxiety.

ICD-10 defines the characteristic symptoms as:

- **Mental tension:** worry, apprehension, feeling tense or nervous, poor concentration
- **Physical tension:** restlessness, headache, tremor, inability to relax
- **Physical arousal:** dizziness, sweating, a fast or pounding heart, dry mouth, stomach pains

People with GAD often find that every day is filled with debilitating worries and concerns, about health, finances, family, work, and life in general. They often anticipate disaster when there is no logical reason why they should. Sometimes it is even difficult to find out just what they are worrying about and it seems that simply the thought of living through each day promotes anxiety.

Sufferers from GAD, however, do not characteristically avoid social situations as a result of their disorder (as is the case with social phobia or panic disorder). If the condition is mild, they can function socially but clearly the quality of their lives is much impaired. Severe GAD, on the other hand, is so debilitating that sufferers find it impossible to carry out even the most ordinary daily activities.

The symptoms of GAD may last for weeks or months and may recur often. People with high levels of trait anxiety (formerly labeled "neurotic"), who have a tendency to become involved in heated arguments and who feel "stressed," are more likely to have the condition develop.

As we mentioned earlier, in the real world people often come to the doctor with a mixture of symptoms that do not necessarily fulfill all the criteria for a diagnosis of anxiety. These patients often show some signs and symptoms of clinical depression as well, although again not necessarily enough to justify a firm diagnosis of that condition. The family physician is likely to make pragmatic diagnoses such as "mixed mild depressive-anxiety state," which, while anathema to the classifier of diseases, reflects the reality of the state of mind of the patients. Such "subthreshold" or "subsyndromal" conditions cause real suffering and require treatment.

Panic Disorder

Although panic disorder is seen less frequently than GAD, patients with panic disorder are often seen by family physicians. The NIMH estimates that 2.4 million adult Americans suffer with panic disorder and, as with GAD, doctors see about twice as many women as men with this disorder. It usually begins in late adolescence or early adulthood.

People come to the doctor reporting frightening physical conditions such as chest pain, dizziness, and shortness of breath.

Careful inquiry should unveil the full clinical picture, although it is a sad fact that many people with panic disorder may visit a doctor (or doctors) or a hospital emergency department a number of times before a proper diagnosis is made. They may go on for years before they learn that they have a real—and treatable—illness. Panic disorder is outlined in the ICD-10 as:

- **Unexplained attacks of anxiety or fear:** Panic attacks that begin suddenly, develop rapidly and may last only few minutes.
- **Physical symptoms:** The attacks often occur with physical symptoms such as palpitations, chest pain, sensations of choking, churning stomach, dizziness, feelings of unreality, or fear of personal disaster (losing control or going mad, heart attack, sudden death).
- **Fear of further attacks/avoidance:** An attack often leads to fear of another attack and avoidance of places or situations where attacks have occurred. Patients also often avoid physical exertion or other activities that may produce physical sensations similar to those of a panic attack.

People with panic disorder have feelings of terror that strike repeatedly, suddenly, and with no warning. An attack generally peaks within 10 minutes or so, but the symptoms, such as pounding heart, sweating, weakness, faintness, dizziness, and so on, may last much longer. Chest pain, smothering sensations, a feeling of unreality (and a sense of doom) are common. Patients often genuinely feel that they are having a heart attack, are on the verge of death, or are "going mad."

Not surprisingly, many sufferers develop intense anxiety between attacks, concerned about when the next one may strike, and knowing that it may occur at any time, even during sleep. Some people's lives become so restricted that they avoid everyday activities such as going shopping or driving.

In about one-third of those suffering from panic disorder, life becomes so restricted that sufferers avoid any situation in which they would feel helpless should an attack occur. Work becomes impossible, social life is much diminished. They are afraid to go out. At this stage the condition is termed panic disorder with agoraphobia, or simply agoraphobia.

There is a genetic component in panic disorder, with a higher risk of the condition developing among those whose parents or other relatives are sufferers. Interestingly, not everyone who has a panic attack may go on to develop panic disorder. It may be a phenomenon that never occurs again.

Panic disorder is one of the most treatable of anxiety-related conditions, responding well to both medication and psychotherapy.

Social Phobia

With phobias in general, people attempt to avoid or restrict activities that provoke an exaggerated fear. In social phobia (also known as social anxiety disorder), it is social interaction (whether at work, in such activities as shopping or traveling by public transportation, or at leisure) that precipitates the physical symptoms of anxiety. These include palpitations, trembling, sweating, tense muscles, a sinking feeling in the stomach, dry throat, hot or cold feelings, and headache. Some sufferers from social phobia, however, do not report bodily (somatic) symptoms, but experience debilitating self-consciousness, fear, and apprehension.

People with social phobia have a disproportionate fear of being judged negatively in a wide range of social situations. These include being introduced to other people, meeting people in authority, receiving visitors, being watched doing something, eating at home with acquaintances or even with the family, writing in front of other people and speaking in public.

Social phobia is a chronic (long-term) condition that can have severe consequences for the sufferer's quality of life. It can stop people going to work or school, and it clearly affects their social lives. Making and keeping friends is difficult.

While many sufferers recognize that their fears are irrational and/or grossly exaggerated, they are still very anxious before confronting the social situation they dread. They feel uncomfortable, "hot and bothered" throughout, while afterward they worry about what other people may have thought of them.

The NIMH estimates that 5.3 million Americans suffer from social phobia. Unlike GAD or panic disorder, equal numbers of men and women seem to be affected. The disorder usually begins in childhood or early adolescence and is frequently, and unsurprisingly, associated with other anxiety disorders and with depression. Social phobics are also at risk from alcohol and drug dependence, since they are likely to self-medicate, trying to use alcohol and/or drugs to overcome their fears.

Other Phobias

There are many other specific phobias, which involve an intense fear of something that has little, or no, actual danger. Among the commonest are irrational fears of heights, closed-in spaces, flying, water, blood, spiders, and dogs, although there are many more. The NIMH estimates that 6.3 million Americans have specific phobias. Physicians see twice as many women as men with phobias. Phobias tend to run in families, and they usually appear during childhood or adolescence. If the object of the fear is easy to avoid, specific phobias may not need treatment. But if avoidance is carried to extreme lengths or involves serious social curtailment, then treatment is advised.

Obsessive–Compulsive Disorder

Obsessions are recurring disturbing thoughts or images, while compulsions are the rituals (seemingly uncontrollable) that sufferers from obsessive–compulsive disorder (OCD) perform to try to rid themselves of those thoughts and images.

All photos are from the personal collection of Dr. Leo Sternbach.

Leo Henryk Sternbach (left), mother Piroska, and brother Gyuszi, about 1915

Leo Henryk Sternbach, 1920

Leo Henryk Sternbach's father at his pharmacy in Opatija, formerly Abbazia, about 1920

Left: Mother Piroska about 1920; Right: Father Michael about 1920

Leo Henryk Sternbach, Zakopane, 1934

In the chemistry laboratory at the University of Krakow, 1934; Front: Dr. Schoenowna, Prof. Dr. Karol Dziewonski, Dr. Jan Moszew; Rear: assistants Majewski, Dymek, two unidentifieds, Leo Henryk Sternbach

Leo Henryk Sternbach in the chemistry laboratory at the University of Krakow, 1935

Leo Henryk Sternbach on Aletsch glacier, Switzerland, about 1939

Leo Henryk Sternbach and Herta Kreuzer, Zurich, about 1940

Herta Kreuzer, Zurich, about 1941

Leo Henryk Sternbach and Dr. Max Hoffer in the chemistry laboratory, building 25, Roche Nutley, 1941

Son Daniel, Leo Henryk Sternbach, and son Michael, September 1949

Leo Henryk Sternbach in Canada, September 1950

Leo Henryk Sternbach, sons Michael and Daniel, and wife Herta, 1955

Leo Henryk Sternbach discussing work with students, Roche Nutley, 1960

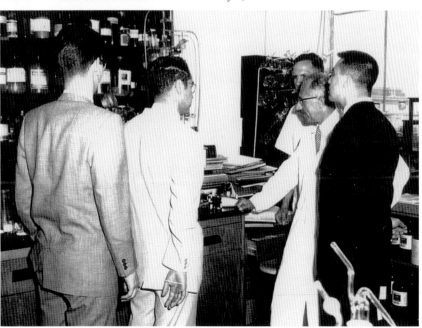

Leo Henryk Sternbach in his office, building 34, Roche Nutley, 1961

Leo Henryk Sternbach's 25th anniversary with Roche: Dr. Gerhard Zbinden, Sternbach, and Dr. Arnold Brossi, 1965

Leo Henryk Sternbach at melting point determination apparatus in his chemical laboratory, Roche Nutley, 1966

Chemistry research team in Leo Henryk Sternbach's office. (numbered counter-clockwise) 1) Sternbach, 2) Dr. Giles Archer, 3) Tom Anton, 4) Dr. William Zally, 5) Tom Flynn, 6) Dr. Ed Garcia, 7) Dr. George Field, 8) Dr. Arthur Stempel, 9) Dr. Werner Metlesics, 10) Dr. Paul Levitan

Leo Henryk Sternbach accepting award for Valium from Mr. Lindner on behalf of Roche, 1970

*Leo Henryk Sternbach in the
chemistry laboratory, 1970*

Leo Henryk Sternbach's speech after receiving honorary degree from the University of Vienna, 1971

Leo Henryk Sternbach giving a lecture at BASF in Germany, 1974

Leo Henryk Sternbach and son
Michael at Roche Nutley, 1975

Departmental group: Seated:
Diane Trybulski, Earl Reeder,
Barbara Sluboski; Rear:
Leo Henryk Sternbach,
Dr. Ian Fryer, 1977

Leo Henryk Sternbach with Dr.
Schweikert at Waikiki receiving
American Clinical Chemistry Award for
"Creativity in Chemistry," 1979

Leo Henryk Sternbach on his way to
work, Nutley, about 1979

*Leo Henryk Sternbach lecturing at
American Psychiatric Association
meeting, San Francisco, 1980*

*Leo Henryk Sternbach receiving
John Scott Medal from Dr. Randall
Whaley of the Philadelphia Board
of Directors of City Trusts, at a
meeting of the Sigma Xi Scientific
Research Society, 1982*

Leo Henryk Sternbach at his 80th birthday with Roche President and CEO Irwin Lerner, 1988

Leo Henryk Sternbach taken at New Jersey Inventors Hall of Fame, 1989

Front: Emily (daughter of Daniel and Wivi Sternbach), Leo Henryk Sternbach, Alexandra (daughter of Michael and Rosemary Sternbach); Rear: Daniel Sternbach, Michael Sternbach, Rosemary Sternbach, Wivi Sternbach, Michael Sternbach (son of Michael and Rosemary Sternbach), Herta Sternbach, at Dr. Sternbach's 90th birthday, May 1998, in New Jersey

Leo Henryk Sternbach at his office at Roche Nutley, 1999. Photograph by Rolf Lyssy

Approximately 3.3 million Americans suffer from OCDs, according to the NIMH, with men and women suffering equally. The condition can often start in childhood (one-third of cases), although it may first occur in adolescence or early adulthood. There is some evidence that it runs in families.

The NIMH sums up the condition well:

You may be obsessed with germs or dirt, so you wash your hands over and over. You may be filled with doubt and feel the need to check things repeatedly. You may have frequent thoughts of violence, and fear that you will harm people close to you. You may spend long periods touching things or counting; you may be preoccupied by order or symmetry; you may have persistent thoughts of performing sexual acts that are repugnant to you; or you may be troubled by thoughts that are against your religious beliefs.

No pleasure is obtained from carrying out the rituals in obsessive–compulsive disorder: they bring only temporary relief from the anxiety that grows when they are not performed. Many healthy people, of course, can identify with OCD, in that they check several times that the stove is turned off before they leave the house, for example, or they look at their passport and airplane tickets half-a-dozen times before leaving on vacation. With OCD, however, the ritual activities consume at least an hour a day, often more, and they interfere with normal everyday life.

Other anxiety orders, and depression, can accompany this disorder and there is again a danger of alcohol- and/or drug-dependence as sufferers try, unsuccessfully, to self-medicate to overcome their fears.

Posttraumatic Stress Disorder

Posttraumatic stress disorder (PTSD) is the consequence of an extremely shocking life event, often related to a catastrophe of one kind or another. Examples include plane, train, or motor-vehicle crashes; natural disasters (earthquake, flood, famine, etc.); or killings and/or atrocities associated with war. Violent attacks, including rape and mugging, are also common causes of the condition.

The event that precipitates the condition, however, may not have happened to the sufferers themselves, but to somebody emotionally close to them. It might even be triggered by the witnessing of an event in which there is large loss of life and destruction (the events of September 11, 2001, spring immediately to mind).

PTSD sufferers feel overwhelmed by the memory of the event and are unable to cope with it. They are intensely preoccupied with the event, and many sufferers repeatedly relive the trauma, either in nightmares or in disturbing recollections during the day. Sleep problems are common, as is a feeling of numbness or detachment. Sufferers from this disorder may also have trouble feeling affectionate; they feel irritable and more aggressive that they did before the event.

If traumatized people who have been in, or witnessed, dreadful events *do* suffer from PTSD (and many of them do not), the symptoms usually start within 3 months of the event. PTSD is diagnosed only if the symptoms outlined above last for more than a month.

The NIMH estimates that this disorder affects 5.2 million adult Americans, and women are more likely than men to be seen by physicians. It can occur at any age, including childhood, and there is some evidence that PTSD runs in families. Other anxiety disorders and depression frequently accompany this disorder.

The course of the illness varies: some people recover within 6 months; for others recovery takes longer and for some the condition becomes chronic, that is, it continues for a long time.

Adjustment Disorders and Acute Stress Disorder

In adjustment disorders patients feel overwhelmed or unable to cope with stressful life events. They may experience stress-related physical symptoms such as insomnia, headache, abdominal pain, chest pain, and palpitations.

There is a short-term phase, labeled *acute stress disorder*, that lasts a few days to a week, while *chronic adjustment disorder* may last weeks or even months.

These disorders arise from an acute reaction to a recent stressful or traumatic event. The event results in extreme distress and/or a continuing preoccupation with the event in question. The symptoms may be primarily somatic (that is, bodily reactions such as a pounding heart, sweating, feeling dizzy, and so on), but other symptoms, such as low or sad mood, anxiety, worry, and feeling unable to cope, may also be present.

Somatoform Disorders

In somatoform and somatization disorders, patients report almost any physical symptom, and often multiple symptoms are described, which may change over time. Yet no organic cause can be found for the symptoms. These conditions are often described as "psychosomatic," and they are very time-consuming and difficult to treat. Long-term and complex therapy is usually needed.

The typical features of somatoform disorders are:

- Various physical symptoms without physical explanation
- Frequent medical visits in spite of negative findings
- Worries about having a physical illness and inability to understand that no organic cause is present
- Association with depression and anxiety

Sleep Disorders

Sleep disorders are very common and cause many problems. Lack of sleep not only distresses people, its daytime effects also sometimes disable them, interfering with their work and their social activities. Lost productivity costs billions of dollars a year. Not getting enough sleep and the consequent overtiredness can also be dangerous. It can lead to fatal road accidents: falling asleep while driving probably causes as many deaths on the road as drinking alcohol and driving. Lack of sleep has also been implicated in many human-made disasters, such as the Exxon *Valdez* oil tanker grounding, the Bhopal explosion, and the *Challenger* shuttle disaster.

According to the U.S. National Institute of Neurological Disorders and Stroke, (NINDS) at least 40 million Americans suffer each year from chronic, long-term sleep disorders and an additional 20 million experience occasional sleeping problems. Again, there is no reason to suppose that prevalence rates are significantly different elsewhere, especially in the developed world.

People with sleeping problems usually report:

- Difficulty falling asleep
- Restless or unrefreshing sleep
- Frequent or prolonged periods of wakefulness and, most importantly,
- Feeling tired, sleepy, and unable to achieve optimal activity and work the following day.

Sleep disorders are usually categorized as primary or secondary. Primary sleep disorders may arise from a variety of causes, such as stressful life events, acute physical illness, chronic pain or changes in schedule or working patterns (such as shift work). They are usually short-term.

Secondary sleep problems, on the other hand, are generally more persistent. They may be caused by underlying psychiatric conditions, such as depression or GAD, or by physical problems such as sleep apnea.

All in all, more than 70 sleep disorders have been described, the most common being insomnia, sleep apnea, and restless legs syndrome. Most can be managed effectively once they have been correctly diagnosed. It is important always to remember that sleep disorder is not, in itself, an illness, but rather is a symptom that indicates that something else is wrong with the patient.

Almost everyone has suffered from occasional short-term insomnia, with jet-lag, work or family stress, and eating the wrong sort of food among the many precipitating factors. Insomnia tends to increase with age, and it affects about 40% of women and 30% of men. Mild insomnia can often be prevented or cured by learning good sleeping habits, while more severe insomnia benefits greatly from the short-term use of benzodiazepine sleeping pills, which will be discussed below.

Sleep apnea means interrupted breathing in sleep. The commonest type, obstructive sleep apnea, is caused by a temporary collapse of the windpipe (because of fat build-up or loss of muscle tone) when the muscles relax during sleep. It is usually, although not invariably, associated with loud snoring. The collapsed windpipe blocks the airflow and the brain responds to falling oxygen levels to awaken the person enough to tighten the upper airway muscles and open the windpipe. There often is a short snort or gasp, the person falls back to sleep and probably begins snoring again. This cycle can be repeated hundreds of times a night and it leaves the sufferer continually sleepy during the next day.

Personality changes, such as daytime irritability and even depression may occur. Sleep apnea is also linked to an increased risk of heart attacks and stroke, and those who suffer from this condition are two to three times more likely to have car accidents than the average person. An estimated 18 million Americans suffer from sleep apnea, though few of them have had the problem diagnosed.

Restless legs syndrome (RLS) runs in families and is characterized by unpleasant crawling, tickling, or tingling sensations in the legs and feet, and an urge to move them to obtain relief. It can lead to constant leg movement during the day and insomnia at night. It is rapidly emerging as one of the most common sleep disorders, especially among older people. Some 12 million Americans are believed to be affected.

Many patients with RLS also suffer from periodic limb-movement disorder, which causes repetitive jerking movements of the limbs, especially the legs. These can occur at 20- to 40-second intervals and repeatedly awake the sleeping sufferer.

The Benzodiazepine Revolution

The benzodiazepines revolutionized the treatment of anxiety and related disorders. They brought, and continue to bring, rapid relief from the symptoms of many of the debilitating and disabling conditions described above.

Controlled clinical trials (in which drugs are carefully compared with other medications used to treat the same condition or against inert placebo preparations) have shown the benzodiazepines to be effective in all the conditions detailed here.

Anxiety disorder	GAD, panic disorder, social phobia, (PTSD), adjustment disorders, acute stress disorders
Sleep disorders	Insomnia
Acutely disturbed patients	Schizophrenia*, mania, agitated depression, agitation in medical conditions
Neurologic disorders	Epilepsy, muscular spasm, spasticity
Addiction	Alcohol and (opiate) withdrawal
Other	Antidepressant and neuroleptic induced side effects

Parentheses indicate that evidence is not conclusive. Asterisks indicate adjunctive therapy with other drugs. Benzodiazepines are useful to only a limited degree in depression and schizophrenia.

Note: Benzodiazepines are not recommended for the primary treatment of psychotic illnesses and should not be used alone to treat depression or anxiety associated with depression, as there is a risk of suicide in these patients.

Adapted from Argyropoulos SV, Nutt DJ. The use of benzodiazepines in anxiety and other disorders. *European Journal of Neuropsychopharmacology.* 1999; 9 (Suppl 6) S407–S412.

Benzodiazepines are well tolerated, which means that patients can, and do, continue to take their tablets as prescribed, with few side effects and little or no discomfort. Above all, benzodiazepines are among the safest drugs ever invented, particularly compared with the drugs previously used, such as the barbiturates.

Of course, all drugs have risks as well as benefits and we will be discussing the benefit/risk ratio for benzodiazepines in detail later in this book. In the meantime, it is interesting to compare the benefits and risks of benzodiazepines with another anxiolytic drug, buspirone, and with antidepressants (some of which have also been shown to be effective in some anxiety disorders).

Benzodiazepines in the Treatment of Specific Anxiety Disorders

Numerous clinical trials have confirmed the efficacy of benzodiazepines in the treatment of GAD, demonstrating their superiority over placebo and over other antianxiety drugs.

Even critics of benzodiazepines acknowledge their efficacy. A study by Professor Peter Tyrer, for example, showed that after at least 6 weeks of treatment approximately 55% of patients remained well (anxiety-free) when the medication was stopped. Another 15% had some short-lived withdrawal problems that soon resolved. In other words, there was a response rate of 70%. This is an excellent response rate, not only in the treatment of conditions such as anxiety, but in any branch of medicine.

Even after 40 years of benzodiazepine use, there is only one other drug, buspirone, which can really compare with the benzodiazepines for the treatment of anxiety. One of the problems with buspirone, however, is that it takes time for its effects to occur, unlike the benzodiazepines, for which there is a fast onset of action and quick relief from anxiety/stress. The slow onset (and occasional early nausea) of buspirone, however, can lead patients to discontinue. In one classic study, one buspirone patient in three dropped out.

The antidepressant venlaflaxine and other types of antidepressant, the selective serotonin reuptake inhibitors (SSRIs), have been tested and approved for use (in some countries) in the treatment of a number of anxiety disorders, including GAD, panic disorder, and social phobia. They have their own drawbacks, including a slow onset of action and side effects (such as nausea, diarrhea, agitation, and sexual impairment), which may be serious enough for patients to be unable or unwilling to continue treatment. A further problem emerges if patients forget to take their medication and a discontinuation syndrome of unpleasant psychologic effects follows immediately.

As we have seen, both anxiety and depression symptoms may be present in a patient seen by the doctor, but these symptoms are "subsyndromal"; that is, they do not add up to a clear-cut diagnosis of one condition or the other. Subthreshold disorders might be labeled pragmatically by the physician as "mild mixed anxiety-depression states," a label that reflects the reality of the mental state of the patients seen by the doctor. Many such disorders cause just as much disability and pain as well-defined conditions.

It is up to the physician to try to determine which condition (anxiety or depression) is dominant and to start treatment with a benzodiazepine or with an antidepressant, as appropriate. If symptoms of depression predominate, an antidepressant might be given, augmented perhaps with a benzodiazepine for the first few weeks (while the antidepressant kicks in) before being tapered off. Physicians are also well aware that benzodiazepines are in general not approved for use in depression and should never be used alone in depression or anxiety associated with depression.

In patients with panic disorder, the treatment of choice is to combine drug treatment with psychotherapy. Behavioral therapy, in which the patient is confronted with the triggering situation, is often a great help. As far as drugs are concerned, it is common to combine a benzodiazepine with an SSRI, using the benzodiazepine for immediate relief and gradually tapering it off over a period of about 4 weeks as the antidepressant begins to take effect. The benzodiazepine is then used as additional medication when needed in severe panic attacks. Many panic attack patients (around 40%), however, do not respond to SSRIs or other antidepressants, and treatment should continue with benzodiazepines alone, with careful monitoring to ensure that no dependence develops with long-term use.

A number of trials have shown that benzodiazepines can be effective in the treatment of social phobia, but today they are not generally the first choice when there are very marked phobic symptoms. (In general, the more phobic the symptoms, the less effective the benzodiazepines.) First-line therapy is usually with antidepressants called monoamine oxidase inhibitors (MAOIs) or with SSRIs. On the other hand, if anxiety seems to be the predominant symptom, doctors will often find it useful to try the benzodiazepine first. Any drug therapy should also ideally be combined with psychotherapy, especially cognitive behavioral therapy.

Counseling methods, including controlled breathing, ways of challenging fears and confronting frightening situations, are also to be recommended for other phobias. As is the case in treating social phobia, anxiolytics such as the benzodiazepines may be used if the phobic symptoms are infrequent, but they do not get at the underlying causes of the phobia.

Similarly, in obsessive–compulsive disorder, although a number of benzodiazepines have been shown to be effective, SSRIs are now the treatment of choice. Benzodiazepines are, however, useful adjunctive medication, helping to relieve the associated symptoms of anxiety.

In PTSD, too, the best initial treatment is probably cognitive behavioral therapy, although this is not widely available. Drug treatment has often been with SSRIs. We are waiting for the results of new clinical trials with the benzodiazepines, after preliminary studies have suggested they could be very effective. At the moment they can certainly play an important role as adjunctive medication, relieving anxiety symptoms.

For acute stress disorder the benzodiazepines are the treatment of choice in severe cases (milder ones often resolve on their own), especially if the patient has great difficulty sleeping. For the longer-term chronic adjustment disorders, antianxiety benzodiazepines may be used for up to 4 to 6 weeks, followed by a break and then another course of treatment if needed.

Somatoform disorders are often long-term problems; they require complex treatment programs, including counseling and even specialized psychotherapy. Benzodiazepines are useful supportive medications in such programs.

Benzodiazepines are also valuable in the treatment of psychotic patients (notably those suffering from schizophrenia), in whom they are generally used in connection with neuroleptic drugs. They help to overcome anxiety associated with psychoses, psychotic agitation, and insomnia. Benzodiazepines also play a key role in the first-line treatment for the management of acute withdrawal from alcohol (the "drying out" process).

Benzodiazepines in the Treatment of Insomnia

When drug therapy is indicated for insomnia, benzodiazepines are invariably the treatment of choice. They have been approved for the treatment of insomnia since the 1960s, and they continue to be important, safe, and effective drugs. It is recommended that drug treatment for insomnia last for only a short period (no more than 2 to 4 weeks).

It should be noted that when treating insomnia it is also important to discuss sleeping problems with patients and to give them information that may help them to overcome their sleep difficulties naturally. It helps, too, to give careful advice about a healthy sleep routine (sometimes called "sleep hygiene").

The versatility of different types of benzodiazepines is important in the treatment of insomnia. As we have seen, patients experience different sorts of sleep problems: difficulties in falling asleep, restless or unrefreshing sleep, and/or frequent or prolonged periods of wakefulness. We have available to us short-acting benzodiazepines, which help people to fall asleep, and moderate-acting benzodiazepines, to overcome periods of restlessness or waking during the night.

As clinicians, we sometimes have patients with insomnia (particularly older people) who may benefit from several courses of treatment over a longer period. While concerns are expressed from time to time about the longer-term use of benzodiazepines (see Longer-Term Therapy for a more in-depth discussion) there is no doubt that many older patients do well on several courses of low-dose benzodiazepine medication. Such an aid to sleeping in the elderly can help to enhance their everyday quality of life. There is a need, however, to reassess the situation carefully (including a review of sleeping habits from time to time).

Patients with sleep apnea should *not* be given sedatives or sleeping pills. Restless legs syndrome and periodic-limb-movement disorder can often be relieved by drugs that affect dopamine, a brain chemical that helps transmit messages between neurons. This suggests that there is some anomaly in the dopamine system in restless legs syndrome, although the benzodiazepine clonazepam, which acts on another neurotransmitter system, is also effective. Clearly, we still need to find out much more about the causes of this widespread condition.

Benzodiazepines Bring Great Benefits in Other Illnesses Too

Status Epilepticus

Status epilepticus is a serious condition in which a person suffers from severe, life-threatening convulsions (a seizure or a "fit") and needs rapid treatment. Although people with epilepsy itself have a higher risk of status epilepticus, about 60% of people in whom this condition develops have no history of seizures. Although it is not very common, the condition affects about 195,000 people in the United States alone and results in about 42,000 deaths a year. Internationally, the annual incidence of status epilepticus is on the order of 50 cases per 100,000 population.

Anyone with prolonged convulsions needs emergency medical treatment as soon as possible: one study showed that 80% of those with status epilepticus who received medication within 30 minutes of the beginning of the seizure eventually stopped having seizures. If treatment was delayed by 2 hours, only 40% recovered.

In the developed world doctors usually have a choice of drugs to treat status epilepticus, but in developing countries they often have to rely on the benzodiazepine diazepam, which is very effective in the treatment of this condition. That is why it is on the World Health Organization's model list of "essential" medicines. This list aims to contain all the drugs to meet the health care needs of the majority of the population. These essential drugs should be available at all times and in adequate amounts in key hospital settings.

Because diazepam is both effective and relatively cheap, it is also used in developing countries for the longer-term treatment of epilepsy itself, when the more expensive drugs are not affordable or when the standard antiepileptic drugs, such as phenobarbital or phenytoin, are ineffective. Nitrazepam has also been used effectively in the treatment of childhood epilepsy, and several benzodiazepines have proved useful in the management of catamenial epilepsy (seizures related to the female menstrual cycle).

Diazepam is available as a rectal gel or in ampules for intravenous injection. Clearly, intravenous injection during a seizure is very difficult, and often the liquid in the ampule may be made up for rectal administration. This facilitates rapid treatment even in the patient's home and can save lives that might be lost through having to go to the hospital for treatment.

Eclampsia

Eclampsia is a life-threatening condition that can develop in pregnant women. Its symptoms include sudden rises in blood pressure and seizures. Pregnant women in whom seizures develop have to be rushed to the hospital.

Doctors in developed countries may have a number of drugs they can use, but diazepam is very effective. It is the treatment of choice (if there is any choice) in many poorer countries for the control of eclamptic seizures in pregnancy.

Surgery, Endoscopy, Intensive Care

Benzodiazepines are also widely used as sedatives/tranquilizers in general surgical and gynecologic procedures. Literally billions of patients have received them, either as tablets or injections, as premedication before surgery, for the induction and maintenance of anesthesia.

There is also an important use for the benzodiazepines to produce "conscious sedation," in which the patient is calm and relaxed but still awake. This is particularly useful for procedures such as endoscopic examinations in which probes are passed into the body to investigate internal organs such as the airways (bronchoscopy) or the large intestine (colonoscopy).

A further advantage of the benzodiazepines in this respect is that they induce what is known as anterograde amnesia. That means a loss of memory of events that occur after (but not before) the administration of the drug. The duration of this effect is directly related to the dose used, and the patient's normal memory processes soon return. This amnestic effect is useful not only during endoscopic diagnostic procedures, but also before surgery and in the intensive care unit (ICU), where the inability to recall painful, uncomfortable, or disturbing events is clearly beneficial. In the ICU, continuous intravenous infusion of benzodiazepines produces a long-term sedation, enabling the use of life support systems and other intensive care procedures. And of course, the antianxiety effects of the benzodiazepines help to calm patients during these difficult times.

So, nearly 50 years after Leo Sternbach invented them, benzodiazepines remain the mainstay of drug treatment for anxiety and related disorders. Physicians throughout the world prescribe them as the preferred first-line treatment for most anxiety disorders.

The beneficiaries are the millions of people who take a benzodiazepine medication every day, to calm their fears, to help them sleep, to overcome life-threatening seizures, and occasionally, to help them through the trauma of surgery or intensive care treatment. That has been the real medical and social impact of the benzodiazepines and the great legacy of Leo Sternbach's pioneering discoveries.

Chapter 8

A Social History: Putting Benzodiazepines into Perspective

The 1960s and 1970s: Enthusiastic Acceptance

After years of having to cope with the dangers of older sedatives such as the barbiturates, physicians were delighted to have, at last, drugs for the treatment of anxiety and related disorders that were both effective and safe. Doctors and patients alike enthusiastically welcomed the advent of the benzodiazepines.

Their use in general medicine, as well as in psychiatry, increased rapidly in the 20 years following their introduction. Valium, introduced in 1963, was particularly popular: a survey of drugs used in general practice in the United Kingdom, for example, showed that it accounted for 1 in 20 of all the prescriptions issued in 1976.

But their safety and efficacy also led to a general belief, again among much of the medical profession as well as the public, that benzodiazepines were the simple answer to overcoming the emotional strains of everyday living. Their use was not confined to well-defined anxiety disorders. (It has to be said, however, that many anxiety disorders at this time were not as well defined as they are today.) As Dr. Adam Doble commented in his book on the benzodiazepines,[1] this led to long-term, routine and indiscriminate prescription by general practitioners: "Benzodiazepine use became endemic amongst executives, housewives, and the elderly alike, and entered the public imagination through popular song ["Mother's Little Helper"] and image."

Late 1970s Onward: The Backlash

By the second half of the 1970s, however, it was also becoming clear that there could be problems with widespread benzodiazepine use, particularly in situations (such as the ups and downs of everyday life) in which they were never meant to be used and in which clinical trials had not confirmed their effectiveness. In the 1980s there were concerns about dependence on the benzodiazepines in some patients after longer-term use.

Among the most vociferous critics was Professor Malcolm Lader, of the Institute of Psychiatry in London, who expressed his concern both to his medical colleagues and to the public. He worried about the "zombifying" effects on patients; in 1978 he published a paper in the journal *Neuroscience* entitled "Benzodiazepines—The Opium of the Masses?"

In the 1980s, other doctors and researchers, such as another U.K. clinician, Professor Peter Tyrer, also expressed their concerns, particularly over dependence on the benzodiazepines in longer-term use.

These concerns were taken up by the media in Britain, notably by a popular television presenter, Esther Rantzen, and quickly became the subject of widespread public debate, coupled with calls for immediate action by the medical profession and by the government.

There were concerns in the United States, too. An article published in *Science* in 1979 examined "the over-medicated society," focusing particularly on the benzodiazepines, but perhaps the greatest impact came from Barbara Gordon's book *I'm Dancing as Fast as I Can*, which described the sufferings of a patient who had been treated on and off with diazepam. There was no relief from the symptoms, but the patient claimed to have suffered severe psychotic side effects. On reading the book, one of us (K.R.) came to the conclusion that the patient may have been suffering from a borderline personality disorder and should never have been treated with diazepam.

The U.S. Senate also held hearings in 1979 on the "use and abuse of

Valium, Librium and other benzodiazepine tranquilizers," adding to the sense of unease about their widespread use.

When examining reactions to benzodiazepine use, it is also important to look back and try to remember the attitudes of the medical profession at that time. Although the psychopharmacological revolution had started in the 1950s and the advent of the benzodiazepines in the 1960s had shown how millions of people in the community could be helped to overcome their crippling anxiety states, there was still resistance to the whole concept of using drugs to treat psychological illness. The teachings of Freud and his followers, urging the use of psychoanalysis and psychotherapy, still had great influence in psychiatry. Many psychiatrists believed that while drugs might overcome symptoms, only psychoanalytical methods could get at the underlying causes of the illness and, hopefully, bring about a true "cure."

Therefore, it was often recommended that antianxiety drugs be used only for a short time, with long-term treatment confined to psychotherapy (analysis). If we had recognized in the 1970s that many anxiety disorders are chronic (long term) and need prolonged treatment, longer-term use of the benzodiazepines might have been viewed quite differently.

By the early 1980s, therefore, medical concern and media pressure were beginning to act in concert to spur politicians and bureaucrats into action. In Britain, the government introduced restrictions in the mid-1980s, in the form of a "limited list" of the benzodiazepines that could be prescribed by doctors through the government-funded National Health Service. The list removed most of the newer benzodiazepines, such as clobazam, lormetazepam, and alprazolam, which were exciting molecules with specific actions on anxiety, sleep disturbance, and depression. In the opinion of I.H., who was actively involved in the debate about the limited list, the extensive restrictions had far more to do with financial considerations and the cost to the government than with any scientific argument.

In 1988 the Royal College of Psychiatrists in the United Kingdom issued guidelines for prescribers, saying that benzodiazepines should not be used for more than 4 weeks. The Royal College also suggested that the risks outweighed the benefits. It even counseled against prescribing benzodiazepines in a crisis (such as bereavement), since it might "inhibit adjustment" to the situation. Many clinicians today (ourselves included) would think that benzodiazepines were precisely indicated for short-term use in such a situation. Perhaps the British penchant to "grin and bear it" and keep a "stiff upper lip" overrode more humanitarian considerations. (It is of interest in this context that among Western European countries the United Kingdom has the lowest rate of benzo-diazepine prescribing, while France, whose people have often been seen as enjoying a more hedonistic lifestyle, have the highest.)

While the British Royal College of Psychiatrists was suggesting 4 *weeks* as the maximum period of use, in the United States a task force appointed by the American Psychiatric Association suggested that 4 *months* was more realistic. It said that long-term use was possible, pro-vided that it was restricted to cases in which there were clear indications and in which the benefits clearly outweighed the risks.

Other countries had different approaches and were usually far less restrictive than Britain, where media attention, official action, and pro-fessional pronouncements influenced the general perception of the ben-zodiazepines and had a major impact. Between 1981 and 1989, sales of benzodiazepine anxiolytics declined by 50% in the United Kingdom, while during the same period worldwide, their use increased by approx-imately 13%.

There were increased restrictions elsewhere, notably in New York State in 1989. Benzodiazepines became subject to the state's unique pre-scription monitoring program, which means that prescriptions had to be made out in triplicate, with one copy going to the authorities. In the following year, benzodiazepine prescribing fell by 44%, but prescrip-tions of meprobamate increased 125% (compared with a national fall of 9%) and prescriptions of chloral hydrate increased by 136% (no change nationally). It should be remembered that chloral hydrate was introduced in the 1840s and is a very toxic, addictive agent, but all these drugs are less safe, are generally less well tolerated, and have more serious side effects than the benzodiazepines. The dangers of the alternative drugs actually used in clinical practice must surely outweigh any risks associated with the perceived overprescription of the benzodiazepines.

Another curious case was that of the benzodiazepine sleeping pill Halcion (triazolam). After extensive investigations and public hearings, the U.S. Food and Drug Administration, one of the world's most prestigious, and careful, regulatory authorities found this drug to be safe and effective. It was widely used in the 1980s in the United States, and other countries, including Britain.

There was, however, extensive coverage in British newspapers and on television of allegations that the drug caused memory problems and psychotic (mood-altering) side effects. These latter are known as "paradoxical" because they have the opposite effect of that normally associated with the drug.

These effects are known to occur with hypnotic drugs, but the British authorities apparently believed that Halcion produced a greater frequency of memory problems and psychotic reactions than other drugs of this type. Halcion was banned in the United Kingdom in October 1991. In other countries (Germany, for example) no such steps were taken, after extensive investigations by the licensing authorities.

The British authorities cited a study that showed that the incidence of memory problems was twice as high with triazolam (Halcion), than with another benzodiazepine hypnotic, flurazepam, findings that at first sight seemed rather disturbing.

One of us (I.H.), however, was among a number of experts who queried the conclusions reached by the authorities. Examination of the data showed that the incidence of memory problems with flurazepam was 0.2% and with triazolam 0.4%. A doubling, certainly, but these data meant that 99.6% of people taking triazolam (Halcion) did not experience memory problems, compared with 99.8% taking flurazepam. In scientific terms, the difference between 99.4% and 99.6% is not statistically significant. In other words, as far as the mathematics are concerned, there is <u>no</u> difference between the two figures.

(Incidentally, postmarketing surveillance studies in the United Kingdom suggested that the incidence of memory problems with triazolam was actually about 0.1%. In other words, 99.9% of people could use the drug without any untoward effects.)

As far as paradoxical psychiatric reactions were concerned, the British Committee on Safety of Medicines claimed that 62% of these occurred in patients over 60. Closer examination of the database, however, shows 26 of 2,888 patients experienced paradoxical reactions (an incidence of 0.9%). It is true that 16 of these 26 patients (62%) were over 60. But it must not be forgotten that the total sample size was 2,888; therefore, only 0.56% of patients from the sample tested, aged over 60, experienced such a reaction. Thus, one can easily conclude that overall, 99.4% of patients did not experience any reactions.

We believe that in this case there was a considerable gap between the scientific and medical evidence and the political and regulatory decisions about Halcion, which were fueled by media commentaries and individual physicians adopting an antibenzodiazepine stance. Regulatory decisions often had little to do with a scientific interpretation of the data.

The tiny risks associated with Halcion were considered by the U.K. regulatory authorities (and those of Norway and Brazil) to be unacceptable in a hypnotic drug.

As Alan Doble noted in his book on the benzodiazepines[1]:

This tendency, on the part of both national regulatory authorities and medical opinion leaders, to consider the hypnotic and anxiolytic benzodiazepines as comfort medicines, rather than life-saving or disease-preventing drugs, has produced a sharp reduction in the prescription of benzodiazepines . . . despite the epidemiological evidence that generalized anxiety disorder has a prevalence rate of between 10% and 20% of the population.

The vast majority of national regulatory authorities, however, including the Food and Drug Administration, allowed the drug to be marketed freely and saw much of the furor as media-driven and nonscientific.

Also of concern in the 1980s, and also much publicized by the media, was the apparently growing problem of benzodiazepine abuse—that is, people using these drugs for nonmedical purposes. As we shall see in the next section, there is a potential for abuse of the benzodiazepines, but they are abused almost entirely by people who have a history of abusing *other* drugs, particularly opioid- and alcohol-dependent individuals. Also, benzodiazepines are some of the only drugs that alleviate the psychological and physical distress in patients withdrawing from narcotics, under medical treatment programs.

1990s and Onward: The Pendulum Swings

With hindsight, we believe that there was some overenthusiastic prescribing of the benzodiazepines in the 1970s and 1980s. While the overwhelming majority of patients receiving benzodiazepines got the right medicines for the right reasons, they were sometimes prescribed for people who did not really need them. In some instances the benzodiazepines were used in inappropriate doses or for inappropriately long periods of time.

By the early 1990s, however, the pendulum of opinion on benzodiazepine use had swung too far in the opposite direction, as was shown in a report from a Task Force set up by the World Psychiatric Association, published in 1993.

Data from the United States and Europe on the use of the benzodiazepines were examined. For the United States, data from the

National Household Surveys on drug use in 1979 and 1990 were compared. There was a significant decline in benzodiazepine use and, said the Task Force, "the decline has come mainly at the expense of people who clearly merit psychiatric treatment." Furthermore, the Task Force report stated: "The decline has not been compensated for by the use of other medication or non-drug therapies." It argued that the decline took place against a background of significant underutilization of the benzodiazepines. Even in 1979 and certainly in 1990, use rates were very low "relative to the proportion of the population with defined clinical need."

Analysis of similar surveys in European countries between 1981 and 1990 found wide variation in rates of use, but there was a decline in the use of antianxiety drugs (mainly benzodiazepines) in seven of the nine countries for which data on trends were available. The World Psychiatric Association report noted that over this period there had been considerable pressure in many countries to reduce benzodiazepine use. It said: "Although well intended, such judgements may be misguided and, on a benefit/risk basis, have undesirable and unanticipated negative consequences for those who are clearly in need of psychiatric treatment."

Recent epidemiological surveys also confirm that:

- Most patients treated with benzodiazepines have levels of distress that justify their use.
- Many people with substantial distress do not receive psychotherapeutic medication of any kind.

In other words, too many patients are being denied a safe and effective treatment for real, life-disabling illnesses. Many people with anxiety disorders are not being treated at all, or if they are, they are being given medications that are less effective, less well tolerated, and often, much more dangerous than the benzodiazepines.

Putting Benzodiazepine Concerns into Perspective

Dependence

The medical use of benzodiazepines and benzodiazepine-like medicines may lead to the development of physical and psychological dependence. The risk of dependence developing increases with the dose and duration of treatment; it is also greater in predisposed patients who have a history of alcohol or drug abuse.

Patients especially at risk from dependence are those with:

- A history of addiction
- Chronic physical illness, especially if associated with pain
- Dysthymia (long-term mild depression) and those with personality disorders
- Chronic sleep disorders

Benzodiazepine dependence shows itself in withdrawal symptoms that occur when the treatment is stopped abruptly.

Withdrawal Syndrome

It is important to distinguish between "withdrawal syndrome" and "discontinuation effects." The latter are abrupt (such as when a patient forgets to take the drug) and can be severe. Gradual withdrawal of the medication usually has no significant clinical consequences.

Nonetheless, withdrawal symptoms can, and do, occur. When they do, they are generally taken to indicate some dependence on the drug. Withdrawal symptoms can range from physical symptoms, such as loss of appetite, nausea, diarrhea, headaches, and muscle aches, to a variety of "psychological" effects, such as anxiety (nervousness), depressed mood, irritability, insomnia, lack of energy, dizziness, difficulty in concentrating or remembering, and a feeling of depersonalization. Some of these symptoms might be present to a minor degree; others may not be present at all. (We should also remember that patients are likely to become "unhappy" when they are no longer receiving a medication that they know is helpful.)

In severe, and very rare, cases, symptoms might include hallucinations or epileptic seizures. Seizures are highly unlikely to occur in patients who have used benzodiazepines at therapeutic doses, even for long periods, when the dose is gradually tapered off.

Withdrawal symptoms are more likely to occur if:

- The benzodiazepine has been taken in regular dosage for long periods
- Higher dosages have been used
- The drug is stopped suddenly
- A benzodiazepine with a short-half life has been taken

The withdrawal syndrome is most likely to occur when there is a rapid fall in blood benzodiazepine concentrations and it seems that this is associated with an altered sensitivity of benzodiazepine receptors in the brain. So withdrawal symptoms can best be avoided by a gradual reduction of dosage.

Patients who are treated for only a few weeks rarely have such symptoms when their medication is stopped, so the first strategy used by clinicians to minimize the risk of withdrawal problems is to use short-term or intermittent treatment for anxiety episodes. In generalized anxiety disorder and some other illnesses, however, patients may often need longer-term treatment for their conditions. But the initial treatment period should not exceed 8 weeks, including the tapering-off period. Then there should be a reevaluation of the situation.

It is also important to recognize (and tell the patient) the difference between "rebound phenomena" and withdrawal symptoms, as discussed below.

Rebound Phenomena

Rebound phenomena are a temporary return of the original symptoms of anxiety after treatment is stopped. By definition, they reach a severity level higher than before treatment. They usually disappear within 7 to 14 days and, again, they seem less likely to appear if doses are gradually tapered off.

Dependence: What the Experts Think

While official pronouncements and guidelines clearly influence the ways doctors prescribe drugs, they are also interested in the opinions and expertise of other members of the profession, especially when they have specialized knowledge in a particular area of medicine. There is a vast reservoir of clinical experience from all over the world, but it has been largely untapped, because the opinions of experts have not been systematically gathered or widely disseminated.

As far as the anxiety disorders are concerned, this problem has been largely overcome by international surveys carried out by Dr. E.H. Uhlenhuth, Professor of Psychiatry at the University of New Mexico School of Medicine in Albuquerque. In 1997 Prof. Uhlenhuth and his colleagues obtained the verdicts on benzodiazepine use and its benefits and risks from a panel of 73 psychiatrists with internationally recognized expertise in clinical psychopharmacology and pharmacotherapy.

More than two-thirds of the experts (68%) agreed that therapeutic dose dependence is not a major clinical problem, even in longer-term use. Almost 9 of 10 of them (89%) said that gradually tapering the dose greatly reduced withdrawal symptoms. The experts agreed that benzodiazepines were less likely to induce dependence than barbiturates and meprobamate, but were more likely to do so than antidepressants, neuroleptics, and a number of other drugs that might be used in anxiety disorders.

"Overuse"

Concern about benzodiazepine use in the 1980s also focused on the perception that they are overprescribed or overused. As stated earlier, we believe that there was some overenthusiastic prescribing of the benzodiazepines in the 1970s and 1980s, but today the evidence suggests that the opposite is the case. Prof. Uhlenhuth and his colleagues have shown in careful studies that most patients treated with benzodiazepines have levels of distress that justify their use. Far from revealing overprescription, these studies suggest that many people with substantial distress do not receive psychotherapeutic medication of any kind. This suggests that there is widespread undertreatment, not overuse.

When those who need benzodiazepines *do* receive them, other surveys show that the great majority of patients use them only occasionally or for short periods.

Benzodiazepine Abuse

The benzodiazepines are abused almost entirely by people who have histories of abusing other drugs, particularly those who are dependent on opioid drugs (derivatives of opium) such as heroin. Many heroin (and other narcotic) users take benzodiazepines to help them "come down" from these drugs.

In order to put the abuse of benzodiazepines, into a proper social perspective, we need first to consider the abuse of drugs in general. When the facts are examined it can be seen just how small a role benzodiazepines play in this story.

Worldwide Drug Scene

It is notoriously difficult to tease out the true facts relating to drug abuse in general among the plethora of anecdotal evidence and media hype, but one of us (J.A.C.S.) has recently attempted to do just that by making an in-depth analysis of the available data on worldwide abuse of illicit drugs and licit ones (that is, those available on prescription or "over the counter"). This analysis was published in the medical journal *Human Psychopharmacology, Clinical and Experimental* in 2002.[2]

In Prof. Costa e Silva's report, the latest available evidence on the abuse of drugs on a global basis, using United Nations documentation, was examined. In addition, more detailed evidence from the United States and Europe, which also looked at the consequences of drug abuse (in terms of sickness and death) was analyzed. To achieve some continuity, data for the years 1995 to 1997 (the latest year for which all the sources were able to provide full statistics) were examined, to provide a snapshot of the drug scene toward the end of the past century. Data from earlier years also provided some evidence of trends.

Of course, the data, particularly on a global basis, are not comprehensive and there is also the problem of ambiguous and incomplete reporting. Nonetheless, the survey, which was probably the first of its kind, does provide evidence of the real problem areas with drugs and the relative importance, in terms of social and medical impact, of different compounds.

In its report on Global Illicit Drug Trends published in 1999, the United Nations Office for Drug Control and Crime Prevention made estimates of the global annual prevalence (how many people had used/abused a given drug in any one year) of drug abuse in the 1990s.

The UN agency estimated that:

- The global annual prevalence rate of all illicit drugs ranges from 3.3% to 4.1% of total world population. 186 TO 230 MILLION PEOPLE USING ILLICIT DRUGS
- The most widespread illicit drug consumption occurred with cannabis products (marijuana and hashish), with an annual prevalence of 2.5% 141 MILLION PEOPLE
- The annual prevalence of cocaine abuse was around 0.2% 13 MILLION PEOPLE

- The annual prevalence of opiate abuse (including heroin) was around 0.1% (8 million people)
- The annual prevalence of the abuse of amphetamine-type stimulants was around 0.5% (30 million people)

So cannabis is by far the most abused drug, although we may perhaps put its use/abuse into perspective by comparing its annual prevalence with that of tobacco, which is more than 30%. And while it is surprisingly difficult to find annual prevalence figures for alcohol consumption, it is probably much higher, especially in America and Western Europe. For example, in Nordic countries, an annual prevalence of 79% to 95% has been reported.

The second most widely abused drug varies from country to country, with the abuse of synthetic drugs, notably amphetamine-type stimulants, both widespread and growing. MDMA (Ecstasy) showed the strongest increase in the latter part of the 1990s. In the Americas, cocaine is the second most widely abused drug, with abuse highest in the United States, where there is an annual prevalence (among 11-year-olds and above) of around 2%.

Abuse of heroin and other opiate-type drugs is much less prevalent, with most abuse occurring in Southeast and Southwest Asia, where approximately 2% of the population are involved (usually by smoking or taking orally). In Europe, the annual prevalence of opiate use (mainly heroin and mainly by injection) is on the order of 0.2% to 0.4%.

Even though opiate abuse may be less common, it causes by far the greatest medical problems: in Europe, 70% of the demand for treatment for drug problems is linked to opiate (mostly heroin) abuse; for Asia, the figure is 60%. Furthermore, about 3.3 million (11%) of the 30 million people in the world with HIV/AIDS have contracted the infection through injecting drugs.

Drug Abuse in the United States

Although there seems to have been little reporting of it in the media, one of the encouraging signs from the United States is that drug abuse overall has halved since the late 1970s and early 1980s. There has been an even bigger decline in the misuse or abuse of legitimate prescription medicines, such as the benzodiazepines.

The U.S. National Household Survey on Drug Abuse, based on questionnaires completed by a representative sample of the population, provides the best data on the prevalence of drug abuse in the United States. Examination of the surveys for 1995 to 1997 shows no appreciable changes between the years, so the latest year can be taken as a reasonably reliable snapshot.

The 1997 survey showed:

- More than one-third of Americans have used an illicit drug in their lifetime (36%; 77 million of an estimated total population of 216 million)
- About one-tenth have used an illicit drug in the past year (11%; 24 million)
- About 1 in 15 people are current users (6%; 14 million).

For many people in the United States, the only illicit drug ever used was marijuana. When this is excluded from the figures, the numbers of lifetime, past year, and current users are drastically reduced. Current use (i.e., having used an illicit drug in the past month) is the best indication of the inherent drug abuse problem. In the United States there were 11 million current users of marijuana and 1.5 million of cocaine, the second most commonly used illicit drug. The current use of any illicit drug in 1997 (6%) was less than half of that in 1985 (12%) and 1979 (14%).

While overall current drug use dropped by more than half, there was an even bigger decline in the nonmedical use of legal psychotherapeutic drugs. The 1997 figure (1.2%) was less than one-third of that in 1985 (3.8%). A major contribution to that decrease came from the decline in the illicit use of prescription tranquilizers (benzodiazepines): current (past month) use dropped from 2.2% in 1989 to 0.4% in 1997.

The Consequences of Drug Abuse in the United States

In his analysis of official data on drug abuse, Prof. Costa e Silva also looked at the consequences of drug abuse in the United States, where detailed information about illness (morbidity) and death (mortality) has been gathered by the Drug Abuse Warning Network (DAWN).

The DAWN-Emergency Department (ED) data show drug-related visits to hospital EDs. A drug-related episode is an ED visit that was induced by, or related to, the use of an illegal drug(s), or the nonmedical use of a legal drug. Up to four drugs can be reported for each drug abuse episode. Approximately 600 hospitals are involved in the study, and the data gathered are then weighted to produce annual estimates of all drug-related episodes in the United States.

In 1997 there were 527,058 ED drug-related episodes and 943,937 drug mentions, showing a very slight, not statistically significant, increase over the previous 2 years. The rate per 100,000 of the population in 1997, however, was 222, which is considerably more than the 167 per 100,000 recorded at the beginning of the decade (1990). Similarly, drug mentions were 397 per 100,000 in 1997, compared with 287 in 1990.

This might seem strange, given the overall general decline in drug use, but it could be due to greater awareness of drug problems by hospital staff (who therefore report them more frequently). It might also reflect a changing pattern of use of EDs by drug users.

Given the relative stability of the data between 1995 and 1997, the 1997 data were again used to provide a snapshot. Thirty-six percent of all drug-related ED episodes were categorized as suicide attempts or gestures. An additional 34% were related to drug dependence and 11% to recreational drug use. (The motive was unknown in 19% of the cases.) The most frequently reported reason for the ED episode was overdose (46%), followed by unexpected reaction (13%) and seeking detoxification (also 13%). The long-term (chronic) effects of a drug led to 9% of episodes and withdrawal symptoms, to less than 3%. (The reason was unknown in 15% of the episodes.)

In 1997 the most frequently mentioned illicit drugs were cocaine

(31%), heroin/morphine (14%), marijuana/hashish (12%), and methamphetamine/speed (3%).

But what about the illegal use of prescription and over-the-counter medicines (and self-medication or recreational abuse of alcohol)? Alcohol is not specifically reported in the DAWN data unless it has been used in combination with another drug. Alcohol-in-combination was present in 33% of ED drug-related episodes in 1997.

Nonnarcotic painkillers were quite often mentioned (acetaminophen in 7% of cases; ibuprofen, 3%; aspirin, 3%; naproxen, 1%). The antidepressants amitryptiline, fluoxetine, and trazodone were mentioned in 2% of episodes.

And the benzodiazepines? Benzodiazepine mentions for alprazolam, diazepam, and clonazepam (3% each) and lorazepam (2%) remained stable over the period 1995–1997, while triazolam mentions decreased by 44% to 0.06% of all ED drug-related episodes. Clearly we are not seeing an epidemic of hospital visits related to benzodiazepine use. The DAWN-ED reports do not attempt to analyze which drugs are used in combination or how many drugs were used in any given episode. But drugs are often used in combination, since the number of drug mentions in 1997 was 1.76 times that of drug episodes.

Multiple drug use is certainly the commonest cause of drug-related deaths. The best estimates concerning drug abuse deaths in the United States come from the DAWN-Medical Examiners (ME). These data are drawn from reports in 40 metropolitan areas and, while they do not represent the United States as a whole, they do provide a comprehensive picture of the drugs involved and any trends.

Drug abuse cases reported to DAWN may be either drug-induced or drug-related. Drug-induced deaths are those in which the death was caused directly by the drug (i.e., an overdose), while in drug-related deaths the ME has concluded that drug use contributed to the death but was not its sole cause.

Drug mentions refer to a substance that was mentioned in any drug abuse episode. As many as six drugs, plus alcohol-in-combination, can be reported in DAWN-ME.

With minor variations over the years, there seems to be a slow, but inexorable trend upward in drug abuse deaths. Those reported in 1995 to 1997 are shown below as reported by the DAWN-ME Consistent Panel.

	1995	1996	1997	% change in numbers 1995–1997
Males (%)	7,078 (76.0)	7,030 (74.7)	7,293 (75.8)	+3.03
Females (%)	2,189 (23.5)	2,328 (24.7)	2,269 (23.6)	+3.65
Total	9,314	9,410	9,616	+3.24
Unknown/ no response	47 (0.5)	52 (0.6)	54 (0.6)	+14.9

The Consistent Panel is those MEs with a consistent reporting history over the years 1995 to 1997. In 1997 this panel comprised 140 ME jurisdictions from 40 metropolitan areas.

This excludes data on homicides, deaths in which AIDS was reported and deaths in which "drug unknown" was the only substance mentioned.

The data show that more than three-quarters of the deaths related to multiple-drug episodes. The commonest cause of death (more than 65% of cases) was drug overdose (i.e., drug-induced death). Drug-related death (i.e., in which the drug was a contributory factor, but other influences, such as psychological state, an external physical event, or a medical disorder, were also involved) accounted for a little over 30% of the drug abuse deaths.

More than half the deaths were accidental or unexpected (56% in 1997), while fewer than one in five (18%) were suicide. In his report, however, Prof. Costa e Silva noted that these figures should be viewed with caution, since in a quarter of cases the manner of death was unknown.

Looking at the drug mentions, we find that narcotic analgesics (heroin/morphine and other opioids are the largest components of this group) are mentioned in more than 70% of the deaths, and cocaine is mentioned in about 45% of them. This is followed by alcohol in combination with other drugs, mentioned in more than a third of the deaths. (Alcohol-in-combination was also the most frequently mentioned group in suicides.)

Here are U.S. drug abuse mortality data showing the distribution of drug mentions by drug groups 1995–1997, but excluding data on homicides, deaths in which AIDS was reported and deaths in which "drug unknown" was the only substance mentioned.

Drugs	1995	1996	1997
Total drug abuse episodes	**9,314**	**9,410**	**9,616**
Total drug mentions	**22,659**	**22,861**	**23,874**
Narcotic analgesics (%)	6,568 (70.5)	6,482 (68.9)	6,950 (72.3)
Cocaine (%)	4,241 (45.5)	4,414 (46.9)	4,295 (44.7)
Alcohol-in combination (%)	3,646 (39.1)	3,470 (36.9)	3,500 (36.4)
Antidepressants (%)	1,425 (15.3)	1,511 (16.1)	1,443 (15.0)
Tranquilizers (%)	1,281 (13.8)	1,440 (15.3)	1,562 (16.2)
Amphetamines (%)	783 (8.4)	819 (8.7)	1,034 (10.8)
Marijuana/hashish (%)	737 (7.9)	712 (7.6)	684 (7.1)
Nonnarcotic analgesics (%)	539 (5.8)	513 (5.5)	553 (5.8)
Diphenhydramine (Benadryl) (%)	471 (5.1)	429 (4.6)	521 (5.4)
Barbiturate sedatives (%)	393 (4.2)	408 (4.3)	423 (4.4)
Hallucinogens (%)	197 (2.1)	94 (1.0)	83 (0.9)
Antipsychotics (%)	178 (1.9)	198 (2.1)	206 (2.1)
Inhalants/solvents/aerosols (%)	128 (1.4)	168 (1.8)	135 (1.4)
Nonbarbiturate sedatives (%)	124 (1.3)	149 (1.6)	162 (1.7)
All other named drugs (%)	1,936 (20.8)	2,049 (21.8)	2,280 (23.7)
Unknown (%)	12 (0.1)	5 (0.10)	43 (0.4)

% refers to the percentage of total drug abuse episodes in which the drug or drug class is mentioned.

Source: Drug Abuse Warning Network Annual Medical Examiner Data 1997.

It can be seen that the next biggest groups of drugs mentioned are antidepressants and tranquilizers, each mentioned in about 15% of the deaths. This might at first sight seem alarming, until it is realized that these groups of drugs are rarely seen alone. In fact, in 1997 the benzodiazepines were used in combination with other drugs in 98% of the incidents in which they were involved.

As Prof. Costa e Silva reported: "In no fewer than 61.6% of the cases involving benzodiazepines in 1997, three or more other drugs were used as well. In 24.8% of the cases, two other drugs were mentioned; in 11.5%, one other drug."[2]

Illicit Drug Use in Europe

Data from the European Monitoring Centre for Drugs and Drug Addiction were also examined in Prof. Costa e Silva's paper. The commonest drug of abuse, again, was cannabis, followed by the amphetamines. Ecstasy had been used by 0.5% to 3% of adults in Europe. Cocaine abuse was low compared with the United States, although it was rising in the years 1995 to 1997. While heroin abuse was also low, it continued to pose a major threat to public health.

The number of acute drug-related deaths in Europe are generally stable or decreasing, after increases in the 1980s and early 1990s. Most cases of death involve opiates, although other drugs, such as alcohol and benzodiazepines are frequently found in combination. Deaths related to Ecstasy or similar substances are widely publicized, but are few in number.

Putting Benzodiazepine Abuse into True Perspective

We have gone into these statistics at some length because they clearly demonstrate the very small role that benzodiazepines play in the drug abuse scene, and even in its consequences.

It can clearly be seen that by far the major problems with drug abuse occur with cannabis, cocaine, heroin, and synthetic drugs such as the amphetamines. When benzodiazepines do occur in the statistics (and it is sometimes difficult even to find mention of them in many official reports) it is clear that in the overwhelming majority of cases they are used in combination with at least one, and often two or three, other drugs.

The international data compiled by Prof. Costa e Silva adds to all the other evidence that almost all the people who abuse benzodiazepines also abuse other drugs. Studies have also shown that only a small proportion of patients entering drug abuse treatment programs cite benzodiazepine use as their primary drug problem.

There is also virtually no evidence of the abuse of benzodiazepines in patients prescribed them for legitimate reasons.

Criminal Misuse

A further negative perception of the benzodiazepines is that they are used in criminal sexual assault. Criminals, it is said, use the sedative effects of the benzodiazepines in "spiked" drinks and rely on the benzodiazepine-induced amnestic effects to make their victims unable to recall the event. In the past few years the media have given much attention to this issue of drug-facilitated sexual assault, more emotively referred to as "date rape." Drugs that have been associated with sexual assaults include the benzodiazepine flunitrazepam, gamma hydroxybutyrate (GHB), and ketamine. Flunitrazepam is made by a number of manufacturers, the principal one being Roche, under the brand name Rohypnol.

The perception that drugs are frequently being administered (to males as well as females) in order to facilitate a sexual assault has led to development of prevention strategies—many of them originating from college and student campuses in the United States, where concerns first arose. The prevention strategies generally relate to alcoholic drinks, so young people are advised: "Do not leave drinks unattended. Don't take beverages, including alcohol, from someone you do not know well. At a bar, accept drinks only from the bartender or server. At parties, do not accept open-container drinks from anyone. Be alert to the behavior of friends—anyone appearing intoxicated may be in danger." The development of dipsticks that test drinks for drugs is also being explored.

Important though these strategies are, few address or emphasize the fact that the most available and widely used date-rape drug is alcohol.

One of us (I.H.) was able yet again to demonstrate this fact in a recent research project. With colleagues, Prof. Hindmarch reported on the analyses of more than 3,000 urine samples from people in the United States who claimed to have been sexually assaulted and believed that drugs were involved. The results, published in the *Journal of Clinical Forensic Medicine* in 2001, were very revealing.

Of the 3,303 samples collected, 2,026 (61.3%) were positive and in 44% of these the only substance found was alcohol. All in all, alcohol, by itself or together with another substance, was by far the commonest substance detected (found in 67% of the positives), followed by cannabis (present in 30% of positives). Flunitrazepam was detected in 11 cases (0.54% of positives) and GHB in 100 (4.9%); ketamine was not tested.

Ian Hindmarch and his colleagues concluded that no single drug other than alcohol can be particularly identified as a date-rape drug, and that alleged sexual assaults take place against a background of licit or recreational alcohol or drug use, where alcohol and other drugs are frequently taken together. Despite these findings, media-led coverage and local initiatives still concentrate on the "drug" aspect of drug-facilitated sexual assault.

In the past decade in the United Kingdom and elsewhere, the ready availability of palatable high-alcohol-volume drinks, coupled with the so-called ladette culture, seems to have generated greater public acceptance of heavy drinking in young people—a special cause for concern in young women. There is reason to fear that alcohol manufacturers, by mixing alcohol with fruit juices, energy drinks, and premixed alcopops (lollipops containing alcohol) and using advertising that focuses on youth, lifestyle, sex, and fun, are trying to establish a habit of drinking alcohol at a very young age. Clearly there are many dangers, not the least of which is cumulative damage to the liver. Another hazard of heavy drinking is also the increased likelihood of suffering a sexual assault.

Safety and Undesirable Effects

The safety profile for benzodiazepines is a very good one. In fact, it is very difficult to think of a safer group of drugs. Unlike the drugs they have (largely) replaced, benzodiazepines are very safe in overdose. In fact, overdose is not life-threatening unless benzodiazepines are combined with other drugs that have depressant effects on the central nervous system, including alcohol.

The excellent safety profile, however, doesn't mean that the benzodiazepines have no unwanted effects, but it does mean that these effects are rare.

Drowsiness during the day, flat emotions, reduced alertness, confusion, fatigue, headache, dizziness, muscle weakness, ataxia (the inability to coordinate movements), double vision—all these are possible undesirable effects of benzodiazepine treatment. If they occur at all, it is usually at the beginning of treatment and they usually soon disappear. Other side effects, such as stomach or digestive system upsets, changes in libido or skin reactions, have also been reported. Older patients are much more likely to experience numbness, dizziness, and difficulty in coordinating movements. Benzodiazepine use may be a contributing factor to an increased risk of falls in the elderly, although one recent study suggests that the use of most benzodiazepines (apart from lorazepam) is not associated with an increased risk of hip fractures.

Benzodiazepines induce anterograde amnesia. This means that someone given a benzodiazepine may remember information before the drug was taken, but there may be difficulties in the recall of information received after the benzodiazepine was given, until the effects of the drug have worn off.

Anterograde amnesia most often occurs within the first few hours of taking a sleeping tablet and it can last for several hours. To reduce the risk, patients given benzodiazepines as sleeping tablets should ensure that they will be able to have 7 to 8 hours of uninterrupted sleep. We have already noted that amnesia can be beneficial in a surgical setting, during endoscopic procedures or for sedation in the intensive-care unit.

Paradoxical reactions such as restlessness, agitation, irritability, aggressiveness, delusion, rages, nightmares, hallucinations, psychoses, inappropriate behavior and other adverse behavioral effects are known to occur when using benzodiazepines. Paradoxical reactions are extremely rare; should any occur, the drug should be stopped.

All patients on benzodiazepines should be expressly warned not to use alcohol because the drug's sedative effects and side effects may be heightened by alcohol. There may also be additive effects if benzodiazepines are combined with other drugs that act on the central nervous system, so doctors have to be very careful when prescribing such drugs in combination with benzodiazepines.

Effects on the Ability to Drive or Operate Machines

All benzodiazepines have anxiolytic, muscle-relaxing, anticonvulsant, amnestic, and sedative effects, with different compounds having each of these properties to a greater or lesser extent. So, all benzodiazepines cause sedation, but often the effect is so small that it is not noticed by the patient. Antianxiety benzodiazepines are deliberately chosen so as to have a strong anxiolytic effect and as small a sedative effect as possible. Benzodiazepines for sleeping problems are prescribed so that there is a minimal risk of a lingering sedative effect in the mornings.

Sedation, whether noticeable or not, becomes an issue when someone wants to drive or operate machinery, or perform any activity that requires, for example, good hand–eye coordination, attention, and concentration.

Scientific evidence shows many medications, both prescription and over-the-counter, can affect driver performance. The use of illegal drugs and the abuse of substances such as butane can also play a part. So, too, can driver fatigue—and the stimulants used to try to combat it. Combinations of drugs, especially with alcohol, can add to impairment. All in all, the subject is a complex one.

Benzodiazepine product labeling advises patients that sedation, amnesia, impaired concentration, and impaired muscular function may adversely affect the ability to drive or operate machinery. Patients are also advised that insufficient sleep may increase the likelihood of impaired alertness.

What about benzodiazepine use in particular sections of the population, notably the elderly, in whom many other factors may also affect driving skills? While some researchers have concluded that long-half-life benzodiazepines are associated with an increased risk of involvement in motor vehicle crashes in older people, others believe that further research is needed to clarify this complex issue.

Nonetheless, care is needed in the prescription of all benzodiazepines to the elderly, and reduced doses for elderly patients are recommended. Again, patients are cautioned that sedation, amnesia, impaired concentration, and impaired muscular function may adversely affect the ability to drive or operate machinery.

So while there is some evidence (and it is not conclusive) that benzodiazepines are overrepresented in crashes, it is really unclear whether there is any direct effect on driver performance. It is very likely that the illnesses (anxiety, insomnia, etc.) for which the benzodiazepines are prescribed have in themselves a deleterious effect on driving skills. Anxious and tired patients would seem intrinsically to be more at risk. The use of benzodiazepines in overcoming these problems could actually be making a positive contribution to driving skills and be helping reduce accidents. We cannot tell if this is the case, for there is no controlled scientific trial on this subject.

On Cognition and "Happiness Pills"

Cognition can be defined as the faculty for "knowing." We might also liken it to consciousness, although defining consciousness has taxed the brains of many philosophers, ancient and modern, and nobody has yet come up with a satisfactory definition. Knowledge and its acquisition are also obviously bound up with memory.

Benzodiazepines can interrupt aspects of cognitive function. In memory tests, for example, the benzodiazepines have been shown to disrupt the consolidation process in semantic (verbal) memory, whereby material in short-term stores is transferred to long-term stores.

So, someone given a benzodiazepine can remember immediate information and that remembered before the benzodiazepine was given, but may have difficulty recalling events and experiences after taking the drug. This effect can best be demonstrated in normal people given a single dose of a benzodiazepine.

It is less likely to be seen in patients prescribed a benzodiazepine and taking it over, say, several weeks. In technical terms, as with sedation, they have developed tolerance to the unwanted effects of the drug. So, the effects on memory tend to wear off with time, although sometimes minor memory difficulties can persist. The clinical relevance of this, however, has not been established.

If we think about cognition a little more deeply, we realize that people with anxiety disorders are suffering from "miscognition." They have an abnormal, exaggerated and inappropriate reaction to everyday information and stimuli. Benzodiazepines reduce the psychological impact of these misperceptions.

Interruption of the cognitive function may sometimes produce bizarre results. (An overblown example might be grinning at a funeral because of the inability to properly perceive and understand what is going on.) But this sort of reaction does not happen to most of the people taking benzodiazepines. They might report feeling a little tired or that their memory "is a little disturbed," but these effects, when they occur, are not debilitating. They are certainly nowhere near as debilitating as the effects of anxiety or chronic insomnia.

It is important to understand that the benzodiazepines are not "happiness pills"—compounds that *make* people happy. Benzodiazepines do not promote happiness, rather they counteract the perceived effects of stress. What they do is restore the lives of people crippled by anxiety and related disorders.

References

1. Doble A. T*he GABA/Benzodiazepine Receptor as a Target for Psychoactive Drugs.* Georgetown, TX: RG Landes, 1998.
2. Costa e Silva JA. Evidence-based analysis of the worldwide abuse of licit and illicit drugs. *Hum Psychopharmacol* 2002; 17:131–140.

Chapter 9

The Scientific Impact
of the Benzodiazepines

Probing the Secrets of GABA

Alan Doble has described the first 15 years after the introduction of the benzodiazepines as "The Dark Ages."[1] Not in terms of the new drugs' effectiveness, which was quickly established, but because we knew little or nothing about precisely how they worked. This was not unusual in the past: aspirin, for example, was used for many decades before its mechanism of action (affecting body chemicals called prostaglandins) was discovered.

It was not until 1977 that it was shown that benzodiazepines interact with a particular "binding site" on the wall of nerve cells (neurons). A binding site is a chemical complex with which other compounds can form a chemical bond.

Neurons communicate with each other through electrochemical signals; the chemicals that facilitate this communication are known as neurotransmitters. There are a fair number of these, the most important being adrenalin, noradrenalin, acetylcholine, dopamine, and serotonin. They work through nervous pathways, interlinked neurons, activating and stimulating them, driving the processes of the brain and the central nervous system (CNS).

The medical impact of the benzodiazepines prompted a considerable research effort into trying to understand their mechanism of action. Indirect evidence suggested that benzodiazepines had an effect on nerve transmission involving acetylcholine, noradrenalin, dopamine, and serotonin, with all the pathways using these neurotransmitters being involved. It was hardly surprising that this led to no clear, comprehensive, and unambiguous theory as to how these new drugs worked. These early observations were in fact measuring secondary or "downstream" effects of the benzodiazepines. The real action was taking place elsewhere.

There had been a key animal study, published in 1967, which showed that the benzodiazepine diazepam (Valium) was active in an area of the spinal cord of the cat, known as the dorsal root, but this was ignored for a considerable time, because its significance was not recognized.

It was not until 1974 that researchers at Roche in Basel, Switzerland, resurrected this study, now armed with the knowledge that this dorsal-root activity was linked with the activation of the nervous pathway system using another neurotransmitter called gamma-aminobutyric acid (GABA).

In a series of elegant experiments they were able to show that the action of benzodiazepines is to amplify transmission along these GABA pathways. (Similar research, conducted independently in the United States at the same time, also established that benzodiazepines amplified the effects of GABA.)

Over the next few years, an explosion of research effort demonstrated that amplified GABA responses were produced by benzodiazepines throughout the CNS.

GABA: The Most Important Inhibitory Neurotransmitter in the Brain

So what is GABA? Most neurotransmitters are excitatory—they stimulate brain cells into action. GABA, on the other hand, is an inhibitory neurotransmitter. It slows the activity of neurons—stops them from being excited.

If the neuronal activities of the brain are likened to a team of excited horses, then the GABAergic system is the reins that make sure they do not get out of hand.

There is more GABA in the CNS than any other inhibitory neurotransmitter. Depending on the brain region 20% to 50% of synapses (the space between neurons where electrochemical transmission occurs) use GABA as their transmitter.

Neurotransmitters work by interacting with a binding site, a chemical complex, on the cell wall of the neuron. A chemical bond is formed, and this in turn promotes further biochemical and functional activity.

In 1977 it was shown that benzodiazepines interact with a specific binding site on the neuronal wall. This binding site subsequently turned out to be an integral part of the $GABA_A$ receptor complex. This was isolated in 1987 and visualized by electron microscopy in 1994.

The $GABA_A$–Benzodiazepine Receptor Complex

Many of the details of the activities of GABA and the benzodiazepines in the brain that follow are based on an excellent review of this subject[2] in the British *Journal of Psychiatry* by Prof. David Nutt and Dr. Andrea Malizia from the Psychopharmacology Unit at the School of Medical Sciences, Bristol University, United Kingdom. Permission to quote from it, for which we are most grateful, has been given by the authors and the journal.

The $GABA_A$–benzodiazepine receptor complex has five subunits, made of proteins, arranged like a rosette around a central core, which crosses the nerve-cell membrane. This core is permeable to electrically charged chlorine ions (anions) that, when the channel is open, pass into the neuron. Once inside, they act to damp down the activities of the neuron. GABA (and other molecules) bind to the receptor and the process of doing so opens the chloride channel.

While there are only five subunits in the GABA$_A$–benzodiazepine receptor complex, each of these subunits can vary in its protein composition. At present, approximately 20 different subunits, produced by different genetic codes, have been identified in mammals. The variations in these subunits could be an important factor in the causes of anxiety and related disorders (see "Molecular Biology, the Brain, and Anxiety" and Figure 9.1.)

GABAergic neurons, producing and releasing GABA on command, are widely distributed in the CNS, and GABA acts on neurons to control their state of excitability in all brain areas.

The mildest *inhibition* of the GABAergic system results in increased alertness, reduced sleep, anxiety, restlessness, and excessive reactions even to harmless stimuli. On the other hand, compounds that bind to the GABA receptor, and *enhance* its effects, help to rein in overstimulated excitatory neuronal systems.

As well as GABA itself, the benzodiazepines and other psychoactive compounds such as barbiturates and anesthetic steroids can also bind to the receptor complex and open the chloride channel (see Figure 9.2).

Benzodiazepines (and similar substances called benzodiazepine site ligands) bind with high affinity and selectivity to a protein molecule

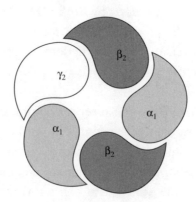

Figure 9.1   The receptor subunits diagrammatically.

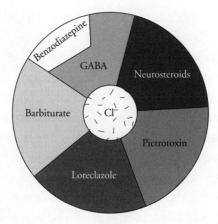

Figure 9.2   A schematic representation of the binding sites on the GABA$_A$–benzodiazepine receptor complex.

located on one of the subunits of the GABA$_A$–benzodiazepine receptor complex. This protein (the benzodiazepine receptor) is an intrinsic component of the GABA$_A$ receptor.

What is interesting and unusual about the benzodiazepine site, however, as can be seen from the schematic diagram, is that molecules that bind to it do not directly open the chloride channel, but rather enhance the capacity of GABA to do so.

So when a benzodiazepine molecule binds to the benzodiazepine receptor, smaller concentrations of GABA are required for opening the chloride channel, the mechanism by which the inhibitory effects of GABA are achieved.

The effectiveness of *maximal* concentrations of GABA, however, is not augmented. So the benzodiazepines act as an internal "servomechanism," enabling the GABAergic system to produce the same inhibitory effect when less GABA is available.

Other benzodiazepine-like compounds have also been shown to act on the benzodiazepine receptor and enhance the activity of GABA. All compounds acting in this way are classified as benzodiazepine receptor agonists.

To recap: when GABA binds with the $GABA_A$–benzodiazepine receptor complex, it acts as an agonist, bringing about changes in molecular structure that increase the permeability of the central core of the receptor to chlorine ions. Lots of chlorine ions in the neuron produce a general inhibitory effect on neuronal activity.

When benzodiazepines bind to their part of the complex, they bring about changes that increase the efficiency of GABA, so the GABAergic nerve circuits produce a larger inhibitory effect. This mechanism of action explains the wide spectrum of therapeutic actions of benzodiazepines and in particular their antianxiety and sedative actions.

The way that benzodiazepines work is also markedly different from other drugs such as barbiturates, chloral hydrate, and alcohol (ethanol), which, as well as enhancing GABA, can also directly open the chloride channel. It is this direct action on the chloride channel that probably makes these drugs more dangerous in overdose. Benzodiazepines are safer because vital brain circuits cannot be damped down over and above the level that would be achieved by the natural effects of GABA.

Agonists, Antagonists, and Inverse Agonists

But the biochemistry of the benzodiazepine binding site is even more complex and interesting. It also holds out the hope of developing new drugs that can have even more specific desired effects and fewer unwanted effects.

In the 1980s, other molecules were discovered that bind to the benzodiazepine receptor, yet have effects precisely opposite to those of the benzodiazepine agonists. They *decrease* the probability of the chloride channel opening in response to GABA and they have stimulant, anxiety-producing, and convulsion-promoting effects. These compounds are known as "inverse agonists."

Furthermore, there are compounds that block the effects of both agonists and inverse agonists. They are termed "antagonists." One of them, flumazenil, is used in clinical practice to reverse the effects of benzodi-azepines, should this be needed.

And there is more: other compounds have been discovered that act as partial agonists or partial inverse agonists. All in all, it seems that the benzodiazepine binding site mediates a spectrum of different actions in the brain. Figure 9.3 shows the range of effects of different ligands at the benzodiazepine receptor.

Why Does the Benzodiazepine Receptor Exist?

A key question emerges from all this fascinating work on the benzodi-azepine receptor. Why does it exist at all? Why do we need this partic-ular molecular binding site? And why are such sites so widely spread among our neurons (and those of animals, too)?

An intriguing paper in the late 1970s in *Brain Research* produced evi-dence to suggest that benzodiazepine receptors in the brains of humans and animals evolved quite late in time. So there must have been some

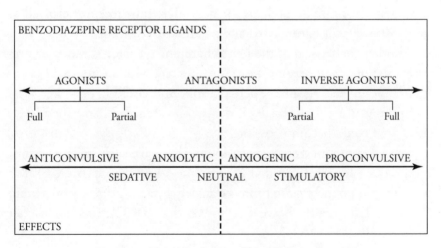

Figure 9.3   The range of action of benzodiazepine ligands.

evolutionary pressures to stimulate their appearance and their subsequent widespread presence.

The obvious answer is that the brain itself produces a compound that helps to reduce anxiety, a natural, internal benzodiazepine agonist that plays an important part in regulating our neuronal activities and helping to keep us healthy in mind and body.

From this it would be natural to infer that anxiety states and insomnia are the result of a deficiency in the production of this compound, just as one type of diabetes is the result of an insulin deficiency. But the identification of an internal (endogenous) benzodiazepine-like substance has so far proved difficult.

It is also intriguing to learn that compounds with a benzodiazepine-like structure have been found in the preserved brains of people who died long before the first benzodiazepines to be used medically were synthesized by Leo Sternbach. Endogenous benzodiazepine agonists can also be found in people suffering from a rare condition, which runs in families, called idiopathic recurrent stupor, and also in another condition, hepatic encephalopathy.

We also know that some plants, notably Aspergillus fungi, can make benzodiazepine-like compounds and that, when eaten, these can be stored in the brain. So perhaps the benzodiazepine receptor evolved to take advantage of naturally occurring antianxiety agents.

Another theory is that the benzodiazepine receptor is there for precisely the opposite reason: it exists to interact with an internal benzodiazepine inverse agonist. Such a compound could help to keep the brain fully aroused, especially if danger threatened. Then, when levels fell, sleep could become possible.

Several compounds have been found that have such inverse agonist properties. One of these, ethyl-β-carboline-3-carboxylate (β-CCE), was the first compound ever to promote anxiety by acting directly on a brain receptor. Later work, however, showed that β-CCE was not in fact endogenous.

Of course, there may be no endogenous benzodiazepine (agonist or inverse agonist) at all. It is possible that the benzodiazepine binding site is just a particular configuration of proteins that fine-tunes the function of the GABAergic system.

Professor Nutt and his colleagues have put forward a theory that the way in which the benzodiazepine binding site works is not fixed, but can alter, perhaps because different protein subunits are created by the genes (see below).

In particular, it is argued, the set point, at which drugs or other compounds bind to the receptor, but have no effect, can move. This may be due to receptor abnormalities, which may be genetically determined. A movement of the set point in the inverse agonist direction (see Figure 9.4) may lead to increased susceptibility to anxiety states, particularly panic disorder. Among the other effects of a set-point shift could be tolerance of, and/or dependence on, benzodiazepine agonists.

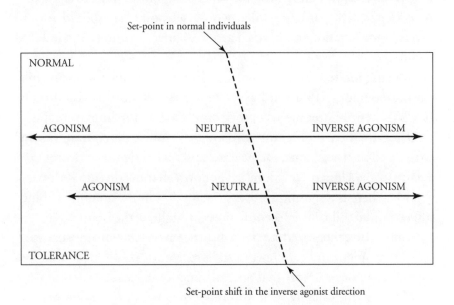

Figure 9.4   *A schematic representation of the effects of set-point shift.*

Is Anxiety Due to an Abnormality in Benzodiazepine Receptors?

We mentioned above the benzodiazepine receptor antagonist flumazenil. Flumazenil blocks the actions of both agonists (which have antianxiety, sedative, anticonvulsant, muscle-relaxing, and amnestic effects) and inverse agonists (which have anxiety-promoting, stimulating, proconvulsive, muscle toning, and memory-enhancing effects). Interestingly, in an experiment in which people with panic disorder were given large doses of flumazenil, it provoked a panic reaction in most of them, while a similar dose had no effect whatsoever in normal people.

A number of explanations could be put forward for this reaction, but the most likely is that in the patients with panic disorder the set point had moved in an inverse agonist direction. So in normal subjects, with a normal set point, flumazenil had no effect (as an antagonist, it merely blocks the receptor, preventing the other compounds from latching on). In patients with panic disorder, whose set point has shifted toward inverse agonism, flumazenil acted as a weak inverse agonist and induced panic.

By using modern brain-imaging techniques, notably positron emission tomography (PET), it has become possible now to visualize the $GABA_A$–benzodiazepine receptor complex in living human brains.

Using the benzodiazepine receptor antagonist flumazenil, labeled with a radioactive isotope, Dr. Malazia and his colleagues at Bristol University in the United Kingdom have shown that in patients with panic disorder there is a significant overall reduction in the amount of binding of flumazenil to the receptor sites throughout the brain.

Studies of generalized anxiety disorder have shown unusual PET scans that might indicate fewer active receptors, or different subtypes of receptors, or receptors that are not functioning well.

Whether this directly relates to mood or behavior is unknown. We need to be careful not to draw too many conclusions from what are quite small studies, but such work is beginning to give us real insights into what might be going on in the brains of patients suffering from anxiety and related disorders.

Other research work, as Prof. Nutt and Dr. Malizia noted in their review, has focused on the role of GABA, and the GABAergic system, in cognition and memory. Studies in both humans and animals have shown that benzodiazepine receptor agonists impair memory formation, while drugs that decrease the function of GABA can have memory-enhancing properties.

In anxiety there is a "conditioning," which involves both the experience of anxiety symptoms and an "association" with events or thoughts that trigger those symptoms. This association is a form of memory, so we can surmise that when the GABA neurotransmission system is inhibited (i.e., not functioning properly or fully) it prompts increased association and an inappropriate overreaction to thoughts and events, which might promote anxiety.

So while GABAergic *dys*function might promote anxiety, increased stimulation of the GABA system could exert a powerful antianxiety effect, by inhibiting both the impact of the experience and the reinforcing memories associated with it.

Again, this is fascinating research, but it is still in its early days.

Molecular Biology, the Brain, and Anxiety

The 1990s have been called the decade of the brain because of the great advances in our understanding of that remarkable organ. Although we have learned a lot, there is still a long way to go.

Molecular biology has perhaps made the greatest contribution in trying to find out just what is going on in the brain, and this specialty has certainly helped us to feel our way toward an understanding of what may be happening in the brains of people suffering from anxiety and related disorders.

To understand the insights that are coming from molecular biology, we need to look again at the five subunits that make up the $GABA_A$–benzodiazepine receptor complex. Each of the subunits is a different protein, and they can be classified into families based on their structural similarities. The principal families have been labeled α, β, and γ subunits. GABA itself binds to the β subunit, while benzodiazepines bind to a site on the α subunit.

There are subtypes of these subunits (α_1, β_2, and so on) and so far some 20 subtypes, coded by different genes, have been found in mammals.

Six different subtypes of the α subunit, where benzodiazepines bind (i.e., make a chemical bond) have been found, and it has been established that different subtypes have different affinities for different benzodiazepines and benzodiazepine-like compounds. Receptor sites that have α_6 subunits, for example, are more or less insensitive to all the hypnotic/antianxiety benzodiazepines.

The γ subtype also seems critical for the action of benzodiazepines, since a γ_2 subunit is needed to produce a receptor site that is responsive to benzodiazepines. The most important, and most prevalent $GABA_A$–benzodiazepine receptor in the brain is made up of α_1, β_2, and γ_2 subunits. These are all encoded from a cluster of genes in the DNA of chromosome 5.

Knock-Out and Knock-In

We now have techniques for gene deletion (knock-out) and gene alteration (knock-in) that make it possible to produce in animals $GABA_A$–benzodiazepine receptors that are deficient in the various types of subunits.

The genes that provide the codes for the production of the subtypes come in pairs. In experiments with mice it was found that if both of the genes that provide the codes for the γ_2 subtype are knocked out, the animals do not survive, but those with only one γ_2 gene knocked out do survive to adulthood and breed.

The GABA$_A$–benzodiazepine receptors of these mice, however, have half the usual complement of γ_2 subtypes, and they are less sensitive to benzodiazepines. Not only that, these mice show symptoms of hypervigilance and anxiety. So we now have a genetically defined animal model for anxiety, which closely reproduces the molecular, pharmacological, and behavioral features of human anxiety disorders.

Knock-out mice with GABA$_A$–benzodiazepine receptors lacking other types of subunits have also been produced. Mice lacking a β_3 subunit, for instance, are hyperactive, have poor motor coordination (they are clumsy), and have spontaneous seizures. The receptor also responds less well to GABA.

Interestingly, these mice are also less sensitive to anesthetic agents, including the benzodiazepine midazolam, providing the first direct evidence that the GABA$_A$–benzodiazepine receptors may be important in regulating the effects of these agents too.

In addition to knock-out mice, we also have knock-in mice. In these mice, the gene that promotes the production of a particular type of receptor subunit is altered. Mice have been produced in which the α_1 subtype is responsive to GABA itself, but not to the sedative actions of benzodiazepines. In these mice, however, the benzodiazepines retain their antianxiety, anticonvulsant, and muscle-relaxing properties.

This work is part of the growing evidence that different subtypes of the GABA$_A$–benzodiazepine receptor are involved in the different actions of the benzodiazepines, so that receptors with one type of subunit may be more likely to produce sedation when interacting with the benzodiazepines, while others produce antianxiety effects, and so on.

This is now leading to a search for drugs that are selective for specific subtypes in the receptor and which could therefore produce the specific effect required, without any unwanted effects.

Molecular biology is also giving us new insights into the mechanisms of tolerance (in which more drug is needed to produce the same effect), dependence, and withdrawal symptoms. As we have seen, there is a lot of evidence that the sensitivity of the GABA$_A$–benzodiazepine receptor to the various compounds that can bind to it is not static, but can change. The set point, at which drugs bind to the receptor but have no effect, can be shifted.

If benzodiazepines are given to animals for long periods, there is a shift of the set point in the inverse agonist direction; this could explain why tolerance to some of the effects of the benzodiazepines could build up and why there can be withdrawal symptoms when the treatment is stopped.

But why should the set point, and the sensitivity of the receptor, change? One possibility is that one type of subunit is substituted for another. When benzodiazepines are given for longer periods, the genes could stop producing the commoner α_1 and $\gamma-$ subtypes and switch instead creating to rarer subunits.

As we have mentioned, there is a cluster of genes on chromosome 5 that has the codes for the production of α_1, β_2, and γ_2 subtypes. The suggestion is that longer-term benzodiazepine use inhibits the transcription of the instructions from these genes. At the same time, transcription of the instructions from a cluster of genes on chromosome 15 is upregulated. The result is that in certain brain regions, receptors with subunits sensitive to benzodiazepines are replaced with receptors that are less sensitive. This could be a way of explaining tolerance. Furthermore, the efficacy of GABA at these new receptors could be less than in the previous ones, so that when benzodiazepines are stopped, withdrawal symptoms might be seen.

Another aspect of brain functioning that is becoming clearer as we use new techniques like these to probe its secrets is that environmental stressors—the impacts and experiences of life—can cause changes in which some genes are called into operation (upregulation) and others are switched off (downregulation). This means that new and different proteins replace previous ones in the brain.

This in turn leads to neuroplasticity, in which there are significant changes to areas of the brain in response to outside pressure. We now know that these changes in the brain can take place very quickly, sometimes in a matter of weeks.

These environmental stressors, which might be physical (toxic chemicals, for instance) or social, may well be the precipitating factors in a wide range of neurological and psychological disorders. Gene activation and the production of different proteins, especially in the receptors for neurotransmitters, could well alter our brain responses to outside stimuli and lie beneath the development of disorders such as anxiety, depression, and many others. A detailed discussion of the evidence about brain plasticity and its wider implications is beyond the scope of this book, but it is certainly an area in which continuing research will not only give us new insights but also, most likely, new therapies for tackling these widespread disorders.

We ought to add a caveat about the work on benzodiazepine receptors that we have just chronicled. The imaging studies are at present few and far between. We need more of them and we need to extend them to a wider range of anxiety disorders. Although we can demonstrate in animals the effects of mutations in the genes that carry the blueprints for benzodiazepine receptors, we have not yet shown that similar mutations are linked to human anxiety. We should also be aware that the effects we see for new antianxiety compounds tested in mice may not be reproduced in humans.

Nonetheless, as Prof. Nutt and Dr. Malizia concluded in their insightful review[2]: "This research should ultimately enable us to develop regimens for using current drugs which will optimise their benefits and to find new drugs with anxiolytic [antianxiety] effects and fewer undesirable side-effects."

On another, more philosophical level, research into GABA and the benzodiazepines has given us a biological, or biochemical, explanation for anxiety and related disorders. Before we had gained these insights there had been, as we have seen, a great deal of antipathy in the medical profession to the concept of treating disorders of the mind with drugs. It was felt by many that drug treatments were merely treating the symptoms, not getting at the underlying causes of the illness. Only psychoanalysis and psychotherapy, many felt, could delve deep enough into the mind to understand the causes and bring about a long-term cure.

The relative failure of psychoanalytical techniques, coupled with emerging evidence that many disorders of the mind may well be associated with deficits in biochemical substances and with dysfunction of neurological processes, is leading to a reappraisal of our whole approach to mental diseases and disorders.

So, more than 40 years after the introduction of the benzodiazepines, there is still considerable research activity into where and how they act in the brain. We also use the benzodiazepines as tools to help to elucidate the form and function of the GABAergic system, the most important "calming" neurotransmitter network to help keep us functioning successfully in a stressful world.

These new insights into the workings of the brain in sickness and in health are part of the scientific impact of the benzodiazepines, since many of the experiments and discoveries we have described above would not have been possible without them.

References

1. Doble A. *The GABA/Benzodiazepine Receptor as a Target for Psychoactive Drugs.* Georgetown, TX: RG Landes, 1998.
2. Nutt DJ, Malizia AL. New insights into the role of the $GABA_A$-benzodiazepine receptor in psychiatric disorder *Br J Psychiatry* 2001;179:390–396.

Chapter 10

The Present—and the Future

The previous sections of this book have charted the medical and social impacts of the benzodiazepines since Leo Sternbach's discoveries more than 40 years ago. So, where are we now? And what of the future of the benzodiazepines?

If you talk to the experts, physicians and psychiatrists with extensive experience in the treatment of anxiety and depressive disorders, you will find the benzodiazepines cited more often than any other class of compounds as a preferred first-line drug treatment for almost all anxiety disorders.

That's what Prof. E.H. Uhlenhuth and his colleagues at the University of New Mexico School of Medicine did a few years ago. In 1991–1992 they asked an international panel of experts for their opinions on the drug treatment of anxiety and related disorders, and they carried out a follow-up survey in 1997.

Prof. Uhlenhuth wrote of this work:

In our view, the three factors that have the greatest impact on treatment with psychotherapeutic medications are (i) the findings of clinical research, (ii) governmental regulations, and (iii) personal clinical experience. The first two are well recognized and form the basis for officially approved clinical practice. Clinical experience is of at least equal importance, yet it remains greatly under-utilized because it has not been systematically gathered, quantitatively analyzed and widely disseminated.

Practicing evidence-based psychiatry is an aim to which we all aspire, but there is little directly relevant evidence for most of the decisions that clinicians have to make on a daily basis for the patients presenting to them. There is, however, a vast international reservoir of clinical experience and clinical judgement that can provide guidance in making therapeutic recommendations for our patients.[1]

The international expert panel whose views were sought was chosen by a peer nomination process, with the criterion of "the professionally most respected physicians in the world with extensive experience and knowledge of the pharmacotherapy of anxiety and depressive disorders." The 73 members selected in 1991–1992 came from 25 countries; 66 of them completed an extensive questionnaire. In 1997 these 66 were sent a short follow-up questionnaire and 51 (77%) of them completed it.

The experts were asked for their preferred first-line drug therapy in each of seven anxiety disorders and every mention of a medication, to be administered alone or as part of a combination, was counted. Their answers are detailed here.

Drug Class	Year	Agora Phobia	Panic Disorder	GAD	Social Phobia	Discreet Phobia
Tricyclic anti-depressants	1992	42	40	30	10	15
	1997	16	20	15	5	11
Selective serotonin reuptake inhibitor	1992	4	6	3	3	11
	1997	34	35	26	25	30
Benzodiazepines	1992	39	44	47	25	53
	1997	39	40	43	26	44

Source: Uhlenhuth EH, Balter MB, Ban TA, et al. Trends in recommendations for the pharmacology of anxiety disorders by an international expert panel, 1992–1997. *Eur Neuropsychopharmacol* 1999;9[Suppl 6]:S393–S398.

Benzodiazepines were mentioned more often than any other class of drugs as a preferred first-line treatment for anxiety disorders, except obsessive–compulsive disorder. Furthermore, mention of the benzodiazepines as a preferred first-line therapy has hardly changed in frequency from 1992 to 1997, despite the introduction of selective serotonin reuptake inhibitors (SSRIs). These have, in fact, largely displaced the older tricyclic antidepressants (TCAs) as the experts' choice in the treatment of anxiety.

Comparing 1992 and 1997, the survey found:

- Mention of the TCAs as preferred first-line pharmacotherapy for anxiety disorders declined by about half.
- SSRIs were mentioned three to eight times more often than the other classes of drugs.
- Mention of the benzodiazepines hardly changed in frequency.
- Benzodiazepines were mentioned more often than any other class of drugs.

These figures are somewhat surprising at first sight (they certainly surprised Prof. Uhlenhuth and his team), since it was expected that SSRIs would have replaced the benzodiazepines. Instead, it seems, a newer antidepressant type (SSRIs) merely replaced an older one (TCAs).

The SSRIs, as well as their antidepressant properties, also promote a degree of sanguinity or a dampening down of emotional reactivity. There is some antianxiety action, which has proved to be of some benefit across a wide range of disorders.

With the exaggerated concerns about the problems of benzodiazepine dependence in the 1980s, which we discussed earlier, there was a move toward using antidepressants, first the TCAs and then the SSRIs, in anxiety and related disorders.

In many anxiety disorders, however, antidepressants are not as effective as benzodiazepines (for example, approximately 40% of patients who have panic attacks do not respond to SSRIs), and they have their own difficulties. SSRIs, for instance, can have serious gastrointestinal side effects and can also lead to loss of libido and sexual dysfunction. The side effects can often prevent patients continuing with their treatment. TCAs, too, can have side effects that impair everyday activities so much that patients do not want to continue taking them. TCAs can cause extensive tiredness, cognitive impairment and increase falls and memory loss in elderly patients.

Furthermore, antidepressants have a slower onset of action, so patients may not see any benefits for weeks. That is why there is a trend toward combining a benzodiazepine and an antidepressant in some of these anxiety disorders, particularly in the first few weeks of treatment. (Prof. Uhlenhuth's survey did not show differing *patterns* in drug use, but he has said that discussions with some of the experts showed that such combinations are on the increase.)

Despite the pressure on doctors not to prescribe benzodiazepines for anxiety disorders and to switch to SSRIs instead, many doctors carry on prescribing them, and they often use them in combination with SSRI antidepressants.

An article in the *Journal of Clinical Psychiatry* in September 2002[2] was teasingly headlined "Don't Ask, Don't Tell, but Benzodiazepines Are Still the Leading Treatments for Anxiety Disorder." It highlighted figures showing that benzodiazepines are still more widely prescribed than antidepressants in the treatment of anxiety disorders in the United States and that the benzodiazepine alprazolam is the single most commonly prescribed agent for mood and anxiety disorders.

The author, Dr. Stephen M. Stahl, comments:

Should those who treat anxiety be surprised by this fact or even be embarrassed about being caught red-handed prescribing benzodiazepines as well as antidepressants?

Or is it possible that wise observations from clinical practice have honed mixing, and matching of these two major therapeutic classes to actually optimize treatment outcomes?

Dr. Stahl urges his colleagues: "So, go ahead and feel less guilty about combining GABAergic [benzodiazepines] and serotonergic [SSRIs] treatments for anxiety."

Frightened to Prescribe?

Despite the continued prescribing of benzodiazepines and the recommendations by international experts that doctors should continue to do so, it is clear that many general practitioners and doctors who are just starting to practice medicine are not prescribing them for their patients as often as they should. Many patients suffering from anxiety disorders are still either being given drugs that are less appropriate, less effective, and less safe and, all too often, they are receiving no treatment at all.

A story involving one of us (H.-J.M.) highlights the current situation. In his hospital, he had a woman in her 50s suffering from depression, which was also combined with severe anxiety. An experienced assistant asked Prof. Moeller: "Am I allowed to prescribe a benzodiazepine?" The answer was that, not only was he allowed to prescribe a benzodiazepine, but that the patient desperately needed it. The indications for a benzodiazepine could not have been more clear-cut. But the assistant, like many other young doctors and like many of our colleagues in general practice, was simply frightened to prescribe it.

At a symposium on "Scientific Reality and Public Perception" at the Royal Society in London in 2000, another colleague told a similar story.

Dr. Spilios Argyropoulos works at the Psychopharmacology Unit in the School of Medical Sciences at the University of Bristol. He told the symposium (which Prof. Ian Hindmarch chaired): "We are referred patients time and time again from general practitioners who are frightened to prescribe any benzodiazepine. They refer the patients to us at the hospital because they are too afraid of what might happen if they prescribe these drugs themselves."

He concluded: "Sometimes we may restrict our patients' lives unwittingly by not providing them with the best treatment. This is a serious problem."

It is interesting that these two anecdotes come from the United Kingdom and Germany, where there has probably been the most antipathy against the benzodiazepines. Attitudes *are* changing, but they seem to be slower to do so in these countries than elsewhere.

Why have residents and family practitioners often been reluctant to prescribe the benzodiazepines to all the patients who would benefit from them? In addition to scare stories in the media, perhaps a lot of their fear of prescribing is because of the impact of government regulations on treatment.

The Impact of Increased Restrictions

Because of the possibility of misuse and the potential, however small, for abuse, it is clear that there should be some controls on this class of drugs. As well as international and national schedules, individual countries have also introduced their own restrictions and guidelines.

The majority of benzodiazepines are controlled under Schedule IV, the lowest schedule, of the 1971 U.N. Convention on Psychotropic Substances. This category accurately reflects their acknowledged therapeutic importance and their limited abuse potential. The Convention recognizes the need for psychotropic substances for medical and scientific purposes and states that "their availability for such purposes should not be unduly restricted."

In individual countries, the benzodiazepines are also generally placed in low category scheduling (Schedule IV of the U.S. Controlled Substances Act, for example). In addition, most countries have introduced their own controls or guidelines, notably prescribing recommendations or requirements, that appropriately reflect the scheduling category.

From time to time, however, particularly when there have been headlines about "date rape" drugs or the fact that many drug addicts also take benzodiazepines, there are calls from the media and politicians for tougher scheduling and tighter controls.

Even if the risks of misuse and abuse are exaggerated (and they often are) how can we reduce them without also curtailing the availability of these valuable medications to people (patients) who will benefit from them? Further restrictions on prescribing, such as those introduced in New York in 1989, are not the answer.

In the case of benzodiazepines and perhaps other drug classes, we have to realize that there are two distinct populations in the community at large:

- People without histories of drug abuse, which includes the vast majority of those likely to receive prescriptions
- the population of habitual drug abusers

As Dr. James Wood has pointed out in the *Journal of Clinical Pharmacology*,[3] the dilemma is that restrictions on benzodiazepine prescribing affect both of these populations. They may make benzodiazepines less available to drug abusers, although this effect is far from certain since drug abusers who also abuse benzodiazepines obtain their drugs from sources other than physicians, through illegal diversion and trafficking. But they also make these drugs less available to the much larger population, who have no appreciable risk of abusing them. In fact, restrictions on prescribing are less likely to affect drug abusers than the remainder of the population.

In view of their therapeutic usefulness and their limited abuse potential, we believe that current national and international schedules for the benzodiazepines are appropriate. This scheduling ensures proper, but not excessive, controls. Stricter controls, which would lead to more restrictions on their use, would mean further undertreatment or inappropriate prescribing of other drugs.

Where do drug abusers get their supplies? There is virtually no illicit manufacture of benzodiazepines: the illegal drug market is fed by drug diversion (the stealing of legitimate products at some point in the supply chain) and by smuggling and trafficking. Manufacturers take pains to keep their supply lines as secure as possible and they also mark their products, and the packs that contain them, with codes to make the tracing of their source easier.

Drug smuggling and trafficking are major crimes, not only because they could put legitimate medicines into the hands of abusers, but also because they have stimulated the imposition of official regulations and restrictions on the use of them. This means that patients who need these legitimate medicines lose out.

Increasing penalties against those who distribute or use benzodiazepines illegally are more effective means to address the abuse issues. In the end, stronger laws and stricter enforcement, combined with educational initiatives, will lead to the best solutions.

The Perils of Replacement—What Happens If Benzodiazepines Are Not Prescribed?

We have already discussed in passing in various sections of this book the perils of replacement of the benzodiazepines. Efficacy and side effects are major issues as far as tricyclic and SSRI antidepressants are concerned, while neuroleptics ("major tranquilizers," mood-altering drugs) in low dosage and sedatives such as the barbiturates and meprobamate are less well tolerated by patients and can have severe adverse effects. And the idea that doctors will substitute chloral hydrate, a dangerous drug introduced in the early 19th century, for safe and effective benzodiazepines is really beyond belief in the 21st century.

Buspirone has also been put forward as the alternative treatment of choice in patients with anxiety. Withdrawal symptoms do not seem to be a problem with this drug. Long-term studies, however, suggest that

patients may not find buspirone as effective and as well tolerated as benzodiazepines, even through a 6-month course of maintenance therapy.
Data from the U.S. National Disease and Therapeutic Index show that
buspirone is prescribed much less often than benzodiazepines or SSRI
antidepressants in the treatment of anxiety disorders in the United
States.

In addition to their efficacy and safety, we should also add that the
benzodiazepines are very inexpensive compared with some of the newer
compounds. The SSRIs, for example, cost considerably more.

Despite the fact that other medications are often less effective, less
well tolerated, may have more severe side effects and can be more expensive, a study in Germany involving neuropsychiatrists, general practitioners, and residents showed a strong trend in favor of replacing the
benzodiazepines with other drugs, even in classic indications such as
anxiety disorders.

In fact, less than 20% of the doctors thought that a typical patient
with anxiety should be given a benzodiazepine. More than 40% would
have prescribed neuroleptics and 60% sedative antidepressants, yet
often these drugs do not have proven or registered efficacy for anxiety
and related states. They can also have serious side effects, especially in
long-term use.

It is shocking that less than 20% of patients with clinically disabling
anxiety would receive a benzodiazepine from these doctors. It demon-
strates again that criticism of the benzodiazepines has been overdone
and has led to a clinical situation that is clearly wrong.

Longer-Term Therapy

When the benzodiazepines were first introduced anxiety disorders were
not considered to be chronic conditions. It was felt that a short course
of drugs ought to be enough to overcome the problem. That is one of
the reasons some doctors felt that when patients received a benzodi-

azepine for 6 months, say, they had become "addicted" to the drug. It also explains why official guidelines in many countries recommended (and continue to recommend) only short-term use, usually a maximum of 4 to 6 weeks.

Now that it has become quite common to use SSRIs in anxiety, however, many physicians seem to want to treat patients with anxiety disorders for years. This reinforces the fact that for many patients anxiety really is a chronic condition.

Curiously, physicians and the public seem always to have been able to accept that some brain disorders will need long-term treatment. Epilepsy is an obvious example. For others, such as anxiety, in the past there seems often to have been an aversion to continuing therapy.

Two major factors are involved in the debate about the longer-term use of the benzodiazepines: sociocultural pressures/perceptions and local regulations/guidelines on benzodiazepine prescribing.

Some cultures seem to regard anxiety states as signs of weakness, rather than as illnesses, and thus tend to trivialize them. There still seems to be an intrinsic belief that, somehow, "strength of will" can overcome (or at least, cover up) the problems and that medication is in some way morally wrong. In such a culture, the use of any drug for any length of time might be regarded as "giving in" to a weakness. It might just be acceptable for a short time, to help through a crisis, but longer-term use would be an admission of social failure.

On the other hand, other cultures are more hedonistic and believe that if medication can help to solve a psychological problem, it should be used. If it is needed for a longer term, then so be it.

Such cultural differences have played an influential part in the drawing up of national regulations and guidelines, because the way people approach these issues is guided as much (if not more) by emotion as by a cool, rational examination of the scientific facts. An emotional response also distracts from attempts to strike the right balance between risks and benefits.

Cultural differences have an effect on *inter*national committees as well, since delegates will bring their own national perceptions and prejudices to international gatherings.

A significant minority of patients (perhaps around 10%) is going to need benzodiazepines for longer periods than those recommended in official guidelines. For these patients such longer-term use is entirely appropriate.

Some of them may experience problems when the treatment is stopped, but the answer is not to withhold treatment, but rather to use it properly. This involves careful management when the patient is taken off the drug—gently tapering off the dosage of the drug over a couple of weeks.

Also, in many cases long-term anxiety symptoms can be overcome by a series of intermittent treatments, rather than by continuously giving the drug.

We believe that several courses of benzodiazepine treatment, or longer-term prescription of benzodiazepines, are appropriate under the following circumstances:

- The patient has been evaluated and diagnosed carefully and accurately
- It has been unequivocally demonstrated that the patient has responded to a course of benzodiazepine treatment
- The patient agrees to a further course of, or longer-term, benzodiazepine therapy
- Other drugs that may have a smaller potential for difficulties on withdrawal after long-term use have been tried first
- All other drugs and other psychotherapeutic procedures have not produced an adequate treatment response
- The benefits and risks of further or longer-term use (including the fact that there may be difficulties coming off the drug) have been discussed with the patient

- Patients' prescriptions are refilled only after consultation with, and careful evaluation by, the prescriber of the original course of treatment

To avoid unnecessary long-term use of benzodiazepines in anxiety and sleep disorders, the initial course of medication should be tapered off gradually (after 4 to 6 weeks) to see whether the symptoms of the disorder are still present or whether the condition has changed. If the symptoms are still troublesome or severe, we believe it is reasonable to prescribe another course of benzodiazepine treatment for a similar period and then to check the symptoms again, using the same procedure.

After two or three such courses, replacement of the benzodiazepine with another drug should be considered, depending on the disposition of the patient and any diseases, physical or psychological, from which he or she might be suffering. Decisions on alternative therapy should also take into consideration the benefit/risk ratios of both the benzodiazepines and the proposed alternative treatment.

Other psychotherapeutic interventions, such as relaxation training, counseling, and psychotherapy (supportive and/or specific, notably cognitive behavioral therapy), can often be integrated into any longer-term treatment strategy.

What we are saying is that with careful management, some patients can receive benzodiazepine therapy for longer periods. In the present climate, however, too many physicians are frightened to prescribe benzodiazepines other than for a very short time. There certainly can be difficulties with longer-term treatment, but with a little care, these can be managed. The alternative is to deprive patients with debilitating chronic anxiety disorders of the effective treatment they deserve.

As in other fields of medicine, there are patients who feel they need some medication to help them with their troubles. As far as anxiety is concerned, this raises the question of whether it is better for them to be on a benzodiazepine or nothing at all. Very often these people will turn to drugs like alcohol to deal with their anxiety, and that is not a good idea.

As far as the misuse or recreational abuse of the benzodiazepines is concerned, our review of the evidence has shown just how small a part they play in the illicit-drugs scene. Yet again, this is often cited by politicians and regulators as a reason for stricter controls on their prescription, despite the fact that such controls will have little impact on drug abusers.

The Need for Evidence-Based Medicine

International agencies, like the United Nations and the World Health Organization (WHO), as well as national regulatory authorities, need to strike the right balance between benefits and risk as far as controls over benzodiazepines are concerned. This is by no means easy, particularly when these issues are in the political arena, but it is very important for public health throughout the world.

It is well known that anxiety disorders are undertreated almost everywhere. Tougher restrictions not only make it more difficult for physicians to prescribe benzodiazepines, but also create a climate in which they are much less likely to do so, leaving even more people deprived of effective medication.

We need also to consider how the climate of opinion and the consequent prescription guidelines and restrictions could inhibit the treatment of subthreshold disorders, such as mixed anxiety and depression. These disorders do not meet the strict diagnostic criteria laid down in diagnostic systems like the WHO's *International Classification of Diseases* (ICD-10) or the *Diagnostic and Statistical Manual of the American Psychiatric Association* (DSM-IV).

Physicians, particularly general practitioners, are often placed in a difficult position because of these strict diagnostic criteria; yet every day they are faced with real patients with real problems that need treatment, even if they do not fit neatly into the diagnostic categories.

There are other examples, too, in which guidelines can be to the detriment of patients, such as problems associated with bereavement.

It is often suggested that benzodiazepines should not be used in this instance, since they may lead to later problems by impeding the grieving process. But if a patient has severe problems, such as being unable to sleep and work, is it right to withhold a benzodiazepine for short-term use?

We need to look closely, too, at the longer-term use of benzodiazepines and not continue to frighten off physicians from using them or patients from taking them. What we need is better guidelines about effective management, not an overemphasis on potential difficulties.

As we have seen, the way in which countries—and members of international agencies—have responded to concerns about the benzodiazepines has depended very much on their culture and on their attitudes toward psychological problems.

Drugs and medicines in general, and benzodiazepines in particular, are often in the headlines, but too often public perceptions of their benefits and risks are far removed from scientific reality. Such public (and media) misconceptions, together with those of politicians and administrators, (and journalists) influence decisions regarding the use of, and controls on, drugs and medicines. They have had a distinct influence on public health and individual well-being.

Decisions on scheduling and on national regulation are often based on *opinions* (of experts, the media, politicians), which are influenced by cultural prejudice, professional pressure, financial gain, political advancement and the need to publish or broadcast "a good story." What we really need is decisions based on *evidence*.

We need hard evidence on the benefits and the risks of benzodiazepines in the clinical setting, together with the real scenario regarding benzodiazepines in society. Data are needed on the positive benefits to the millions of sufferers from anxiety disorders and on the true extent of misuse and abuse—and the costs of that to society. Certainly the new agenda for the WHO is that its recommendations in the future are to be increasingly on the basis of evidence-based medicine.

While the application of such techniques for mental health is comparatively new, we probably do have enough material for a scientific analysis of the use of benzodiazepines (and other psychotropic drugs) in clinical settings, in order that we can more accurately assess their benefits for, and their damage to, public health. One of us (J.A.C.S.) at The International Centre for Mental Health Policy, a joint venture by WHO and New York University, is examining mental health strategies in this way. Other groups are also working on similar projects.

We hope our review, too, may have played a small part in putting the benefits and risks of the benzodiazepines into a proper perspective.

References

1. Uhlenhuth EH, Balter MB, Ban TA, et al. Trends in recommendations for the pharmacology of anxiety disorders by an international expert panel, 1992–1997. Eur Neuropsychopharmacol 1999;9[Suppl 6]:S393–S398.
2. Stahl SM. Don't Ask, Don't Tell, but Benzodiazepines Are Still the Leading Treatments for Anxiety Disorder. J Clin Psychiatry 2002;63:756–757.
3. Wood J. Problems and opportunities in regulation of benzodiazepines. J Clin Pharmacol 1998;38:773–782.

Index

About the Authors

For Part I: The Biography of Leo Henryk Sternbach

Alex Baenninger lives in Stettfurt, Switzerland, and contributes regularly to the *Neue Zürcher Zeitung*, one of the country's most important and influential newspapers. He has written several books on cultural and social topics. After studying Law and Economy at the University of Zurich, he served as Director Deputy of the Swiss Federal Office of Culture, and as Head of Cultural Programs for the Swiss Television Company.

For Part II: The Drug That Changed the World

Dr. Jorge Alberto Costa e Silva, former Executive Director for Mental Health at the World Health Organization in Geneva, is a Professor of Psychiatry at New York University Medical School. He is a former president of the World Psychiatric Association and has served as Dean of the Medical School of the State University of Rio de Janeiro.

Professor Ian Hindmarch currently holds the Chair in Human Psychopharmacology and is Head of the HPRU Medical Research Centre at the University of Surrey, U.K. He is well known for his research on the psychometrics of psychoactive drugs and has published widely on the pharmacodynamics of the benzodiazepines.

Dr. Hans-Juergen Moeller is a full Professor of Psychiatry and Chairman of the Psychiatric Department of Ludwig-Maximillians University in Munich. The focus of his research is biological psychiatry and psychopharmacology. He has authored several textbooks on these topics. Past President of the World Federation of Societies of Biological Psychiatry, Dr. Moeller is a member of the Executive Committee of the European College of Neuropsychopharmacology, Cochairman of the pharmacopsychiatry section of the World Psychiatric Association, and a member of the Council of the Association of European Psychiatrists.

Karl Rickels, M.D., is the Stuart and Emily Mudd Professor of Human Behavior and Professor of Psychiatry at the University of Pennsylvania School of Medicine. An internationally recognized expert in psychopharmacology, with a particular interest in anxiety disorders, Dr. Rickels has written or edited seven books on the subject. He has served on advisory committees for the U.S. Food and Drug Administration and the National Institute of Mental Health. His principal areas of academic interest are the psychopathology and treatment of anxiety disorders, premenstrual syndrome, and benzodiazepine dependence.